W9-BFC-402

The
Origin of Species

Titles in the
Words That Changed History series include:

Words
THAT
CHANGED
HISTORY

The Origin of Species

by Don Nardo

Lucent Books
P.O. Box 289011, San Diego, CA 92198-9011

576.8 NAR

Library of Congress Cataloging-in-Publication Data

Nardo, Don, 1947–
  Origin of species: Darwin's theory of evolution / by Don Nardo.
    p. cm. — (Words that changed history)
  Includes bibliographical references and index.
  ISBN 1-56006-801-9 (lib. : alk. paper)
  1. Darwin, Charles, 1809–1882. On the origin of species—Juvenile literature.
2. Evolution (Biology)—Juvenile literature. 3. Natural selection—Juvenile
literature. [1. Darwin, Charles, 1809–1882. On the origin of species. 2.
Evolution. 3. Natural selection.] I. Title. II. Series.
  QH367.1 .N27 2001
  576.8'2—dc21
                                                                00-009681

Contents

Foreword

"We hold these truths to be self-evident, that all men are created equal, that they are endowed by their Creator with certain unalienable Rights, that among these are Life, Liberty and the pursuit of Happiness." So states one of America's most cherished documents, the Declaration of Independence. These words ripple through time. They represent the thoughts of the Declaration's author, Thomas Jefferson, but at the same time they reflect the attitudes of a nation in which individual rights were trampled by a foreign government. To many of Jefferson's contemporaries, these words characterized a revolutionary philosophy of liberty. Many Americans today still believe the ideas expressed in the Declaration were uniquely American. And while it is true that this document was a product of American ideals and values, its ideas did not spring from an intellectual vacuum. The Enlightenment which had pervaded France and England for years had proffered ideas of individual rights, and Enlightenment scholars drew their notions from historical antecedents tracing back to ancient Greece.

In essence, the Declaration was part of an ongoing historical dialogue concerning the conflict between individual rights and government powers. There is no doubt, however, that it made a palpable impact on its times. For colonists, the Declaration listed their grievances and set out the ideas for which they would stand and fight. These words changed history for Americans. But the Declaration also changed history for other nations; in France, revolutionaries would emulate concepts of self-rule to bring down their own monarchy and draft their own philosophies in a document known as the Declaration of the Rights of Man and of the Citizen. And the historical dialogue continues today in many third world nations.

Lucent Books's Words That Changed History series looks at oral and written documents in light of their historical context and their lasting impact. Some documents, such as the Declaration, spurred people to immediately change society; other documents fostered lasting intellectual debate. For example, Charles Darwin's treatise *On the Origin of Species* did not simply extend the discussion of human origins, it offered a theory of evolution which eventually would cause a schism between some religious and scientific thinkers. The debate still rages as people on both sides reaffirm their intellectual positions, even as new scientific evidence continues to impact the issue.

Students researching famous documents, the time periods in which they were prominent, or the issues they raise will find the books in this series both compelling and useful. Readers will see the chain of events that give rise to historical events. They will understand through the examination of specific documents that ideas or philosophies always have their antecedents, and they will learn how these documents carried on the legacy of influence by affecting people in other places or other times. The format for the series emphasizes these points by devoting chapters to the political or intellectual climate of the times, the values and prejudices of the drafters or speakers, the contents of the document and its impact on its contemporaries, and the manner in which perceptions of the document have changed through time.

In addition to their format, the books in Lucent's Words That Changed History series contain features that enhance understanding. Many primary and secondary source quotes give readers insight into the thoughts of the document's contemporaries as well as those who interpret the document's significance in hindsight. Sidebars interspersed throughout the text offer greater examination of relevant personages or significant events to provide readers with a broader historical context. Footnotes allow readers to verify the credibility of source material. Two bibliographies give students the opportunity to expand their research. And an appendix that includes excerpts as well as full text of original documents gives students access to the larger historical picture into which these documents fit.

History is often shaped by words. Oral and written documents concretize the thoughts of a select few, but they often transform the beliefs of an entire era or nation. As Confucius asserted, "Without knowing the force of words, it is impossible to know men." And understanding the power of words reveals a new way of understanding history.

Introduction

The Two Revolutions of Darwin's Masterwork

Ever since English naturalist Charles Darwin published his landmark book, *The Origin of Species,* in 1859, a majority of people have come firmly to identify that work, and Darwin himself, with the scientific concept of evolution. This mild-mannered, humble, and unarguably brilliant individual became, in the words of Hoover Institute scholar Robert Wesson, "the symbol of evolution personified. Acceptance or denial of the theory of evolution came to be and has remained nearly equivalent to loyalty or opposition to Darwin."[1]

This turn of events is understandable. In *Origin,* Darwin strongly makes the case for evolution, that is, for life-forms changing and developing over the course of time in response to changes and challenges in the natural environment. The ability or lack of ability to adapt to these changes, he says, is a key factor in the evolutionary process. Many species of plants and animals that existed in the past were unable to adapt, so they became extinct; while those that *were* able to adapt survived, often in new forms. And in this same manner, therefore, species that do not yet exist will someday develop from species living today.

No matter how strong the association between the idea of evolution and Darwin's masterwork, however, it must be remembered that Darwin did not invent the idea. The notion that evolution was a completely new and unexpected concept with which he stunned the world and upset many people is a common misconception. Indeed, a number of thinkers and scientists, including Darwin's own grandfather, had proposed evolutionary theories before his time; and these theories had been widely discussed among scientists and other educated people. What, then, made Darwin's theory of evolution different from these predecessors and caused the major tenets of his book to be accepted by contemporary and later generations of scientists? First, Darwin proposed a credible explanation of a number of the principle forces driving the process of evolution, an area most prior evolutionists had only touched on. Second, he provided large amounts of supporting evidence drawn from observations of the natural world, evidence that gave his central theses tremendous weight.

Darwin's evidence was so overwhelming, in fact, that the entire scientific establishment came to accept the concept of evolution in only a few short years. This was a bold development, to be sure. Before this time the vast majority of people, including most scientists, accepted that God had created living things miraculously, or at least had had some controlling influence in their production. Not surprisingly, evolution, which proposes a completely natural, undirected process of creation, had been seen largely as a radical, unsavory, and unpopular idea. By suddenly accepting the thesis of evolution in the wake of Darwin's book, therefore, the scientific community was asserting itself against the powerful forces of religious and social orthodoxy. This daring new posture made science more independent of these forces, more able to stand on its own as a recognized source of wisdom in the modern world.

This imposing statue of Darwin as he appeared in old age stands in his hometown of Shrewsbury, in western England.

But though Darwin's masterwork had convinced the scientific community that evolution was indeed at work in nature, not all scientists agreed with all of his particulars. It is still not widely appreciated by nonscientists that certain aspects of the theory Darwin sketched in *Origin* were debated, doubted, and even rejected by many experts in the late 1800s and early 1900s. That does not mean that these scientists doubted or rejected the idea of evolution itself. Rather, they disagreed about the exact manner in which evolution occurs. Some experts eventually suggested, for example, that it is not always a gradual, steady process, as Darwin had originally envisioned it, but instead can occur in more widely spaced, sudden bursts of activity.

Still, for the most part Darwin's theory remained intact. And as the twentieth century progressed, the theory seemed to grow stronger and even more authoritative than it had been when it first appeared. This was because it was able to withstand the challenges that a stream of major new scientific discoveries presented to traditional scientific theories. For instance, Darwin knew that there had to be some way for parent plants and animals to pass on hereditary information to their offspring; but he was unable to discern the specific mechanism involved. That mechanism, the genetic code (consisting of genes and DNA, tiny particles and substances that exist within cells and carry the coded blueprints for life), was not well understood until the twentieth century. Significantly, the advent of the scientific discipline of genetics did not demolish Darwin's theory; to the contrary, it actually strengthened it, as scientists found and continue to find that new knowledge about genetics fits well into and amplifies Darwin's vision of evolutionary change.

Thus, the theory of evolution expounded in Darwin's *Origin* produced in a sense two revolutions, each of which significantly serviced the advancement of science. The first revolution, which occurred in

A reproduction of the title page of the first edition of Darwin's The Origin of Species.

ON

THE ORIGIN OF SPECIES

BY MEANS OF NATURAL SELECTION,

OR THE

PRESERVATION OF FAVOURED RACES IN THE STRUGGLE
FOR LIFE.

By CHARLES DARWIN, M.A.,
FELLOW OF THE ROYAL, GEOLOGICAL, LINNÆAN, ETC., SOCIETIES;
AUTHOR OF 'JOURNAL OF RESEARCHES DURING H. M. S. BEAGLE'S VOYAGE
ROUND THE WORLD.'

LONDON:
JOHN MURRAY, ALBEMARLE STREET.
1859.

The right of Translation is reserved.

the years immediately following the book's publication, consisted of making evolution a universally accepted idea among scientists, while elevating the status and prestige of science itself. "The evolutionists of the late-Victorian era had their own reasons for hailing Darwin as a hero of science," says Peter Bowler of the University of Belfast.

> [Darwin] played a decisive role in allowing science to tackle an area of study that had hitherto [before] remained off-limits. Darwinism was the symbol of the progressivism at the heart of the new ideology that made science the chief source of authority in Western culture.[2]

Later, well after Darwin's death, his *Origin* did science a second service by providing a firm but highly flexible base on which modern scientists could build and expand. Plugging new discoveries into the live socket, so to speak, of Darwinian theory energized and revolutionized the biological sciences in the twentieth century and promises to continue doing so in the new millennium. Considering these two remarkable accomplishments of Darwin's masterwork, Bowler concludes:

> He was both a product of his own times and a thinker who created an idea capable of being exploited by later scientists with very different values. Any attempt to understand Darwin . . . must first take into account the multiple roles that his name has played within the symbolism of both nineteenth and twentieth-century thought.[3]

Senate
Gort to the Ly,
all intents
he exp
y detail of the
so complete

CHAPTER 1 An Eager Young Naturalist on a Voyage of Discovery

Charles Darwin's most important and influential work, *The Origin of Species,* had a conspicuously long and laborious birth. He accomplished the actual writing of the book in the months leading up to its publication in December 1859. But this stage of the project seemed almost an afterthought, for it was the culmination of nearly thirty years of diligent, methodical, and far-ranging observation, research, and deduction. Darwin was a young man in his mid-twenties when he began to accumulate the experiences, discoveries, observations, and clues that would eventually lead him to his masterful vision of the evolution of life on earth. The crucial formative period of this grand theory was the early 1830s. During these years he went on a voyage around the world, visiting remote, primitive continents and islands, and quickly became fascinated by numerous strange, unexplainable variations in some of the animal species he observed. The desire to understand why these variations had come to exist peaked his interest in the idea of evolution and set him on the long, torturous path that would lead to the writing and publication of *Origin.* Unbeknownst to the young Darwin as he boarded the ship for his voyage into the unknown, he was about to change forever not only the direction of his own life but the future course of human scientific endeavor as well.

The Highest Respect for Knowledge and Learning

When Darwin was a child, neither he nor anyone he knew could have foreseen that he would one day end up taking that fateful voyage around the world; nor that he would subsequently become a world-renowned scientist. Yet the seeds of his thirst for knowledge, and in particular of his strong fascination with the wonders of the natural world, were certainly sown by his parents and early environment and experiences. Born on February 12, 1809, in Shrewsbury, a market town in western England, Darwin was the fifth of the six children born to Robert Darwin, the most respected doctor in the region, and his wife, Susannah. It was to prove a vital underpinning of Charles Darwin's character and life's work that his parents passed on to him a family tradition of the highest respect for knowledge and learning. Robert Darwin was the son of Erasmus Darwin, a noted scholar who had written a number of widely read volumes about nature and had had the audacity to turn down an offer to be King George III's personal physician.

On the other side of the family, Susannah Darwin's father was Josiah Wedgwood, the renowned maker of fine pottery. Wedgwood was also a philanthropist who contributed a great deal of money to educational causes and instilled a love of learning in his children. Young Charles was clearly fortunate to be part of a family in which the adults on both sides were well-to-do and well educated. Unlike most of the other children in Shrewsbury and neighboring towns, who came from poorer families, he and his siblings each had their own room. The Darwins had servants to do most of the chores, so there was ample time for the children to read and learn outside of school; and the latest and best books were always readily available to them.

From this strong family emphasis on learning and education, it would seem to follow that young Charles would be an avid and remarkable student. But this was not the case. In 1818 Robert Darwin enrolled the boy, then nine, in Shrewsbury School, situated about a mile from the Darwins' residence. The headmaster was an Anglican minister named Dr. Samuel Butler, who enforced strict discipline among his students, yet allowed them to work out their differences "honorably" in supervised fistfights. As for the quality of the education Butler offered, Darwin himself later wrote:

Erasmus Darwin, pictured here, was a well-known and respected scholar.

Nothing could have been worse for the development of the mind than Dr. Butler's school, as it [the curriculum it offered] was strictly classical [i.e., consisted of works written by or about the ancient Greeks and Romans], nothing else being taught, except a little ancient geography and history. The school as a means of education to me was simply a blank. During my whole life I have been singularly incapable of mastering any language. Especial attention was made [in the school] to verse-making, and this I could never do well. . . . Much attention was paid to learning by heart the lessons of the previous day; this I could effect with great facility [ease], learning forty or fifty lines of [the Roman poet] Virgil or [the Greek poet] Homer, whilst I was in morning chapel; but this exercise was utterly useless, for every verse was forgotten in forty-eight hours.[4]

Darwin much preferred scientific topics, especially those relating to nature, to memorizing Latin and Greek verses. However, during his childhood science was not yet systematically taught in secondary schools, the common wisdom being that scientific notions were nearly useless knowledge for young upper-class gentlemen and ladies. Attempting to make up for this educational oversight, the boy often took long walks in the forests and fields, observing nature and hunting. "I do not believe," he later recalled, "that anyone could have shown more zeal for the most holy cause than I did for shooting birds."[5] Yet while involved in this very act of killing birds, the young Darwin found himself drawn to studying them. "I took much pleasure in watching the habits of birds, and even made notes on the subject. In my simplicity, I remember wondering why every gentleman did not become an ornithologist [bird expert]."[6] The boy also began collecting and studying insects (although at first he collected only dead ones, his sister having convinced him that killing them for study was wrong).

As Darwin himself later told it, Dr. Butler did not approve of the boy "wasting" his time on such "useless" pursuits. Moreover, the elder Darwin, whose opinions mattered a good deal more to Charles than Butler's did, agreed.

To my deep mortification, my father once said to me, "You care for nothing but shooting, dogs, and rat-catching, and you will be a disgrace to yourself and all your family." But my father, who was the kindest man I ever knew, and whose memory I love with all my heart, must have been angry and somewhat unjust when he used such words.[7]

Darwin's College Years

Angry and unjust or not, Robert Darwin hoped to set his son straight, and in 1825 he removed Charles, then sixteen, from Dr. Butler's school and enrolled him in Edinburgh University. There, the young man was forced to study medicine, in the expectation that he would become a respectable doctor like his father and grandfather before him. But this was not to be. Darwin was bored almost to tears by his medical studies and found the act of dissecting animals repulsive. Even worse was the

14

A nineteenth-century woodcut of Edinburgh University, where Darwin reluctantly enrolled as a medical student.

spectacle of surgery on a human being. One day he had to attend an operation being performed on a child, who was held down during the procedure, as was the custom, because anesthesia had not yet been introduced into operating rooms. The child's screams were too much for Darwin and he fled, horrified, from the room.[8]

After two years Darwin's father finally saw that the young man was not promising doctor material. But Robert Darwin's alternative was to force his son to study for the ministry at Cambridge University, where Charles spent the next three years, as unmotivated as ever with his studies. Actually, it was mainly his theology classes that bored the younger Darwin; for while at Cambridge he met and began studying informally with John Stevens Henslow, a widely respected botanist. According to Darwin's own recollection:

> Before coming up to Cambridge, I had heard of him from my brother as a man who knew every branch of science, and I was accordingly prepared to reverence him. He kept open house once every week when all undergraduates and some older members of the University, who were attached to science, used to meet in the evening. I soon . . . went there regularly. Before long I became well acquainted with Henslow, and during the latter half of my time at Cambridge took long walks with him on most days; so that I was called by some. . .

"the man who walks with Henslow." . . . His knowledge was great in botany, entomology [the study of insects], chemistry, mineralogy, and geology.[9]

After obtaining his bachelor's degree in theology in January 1831, Darwin also met and studied with the renowned geologist and clergyman Adam Sedgwick, whom the young man considered a brilliant teacher. Darwin became close with Sedgwick, as well as with some of Henslow's friends, all of whom were a good deal older than he. "Looking back," Darwin later wrote,

> I infer that there must have been something in me a little superior to the common run of youths, otherwise, the above-mentioned men, so much older than me and higher in academical position, would never have allowed me to associate with them.[10]

The *Beagle* Sets Sail

Indeed, far from the "common run of youths," Darwin was really a brilliant, restless young man whose enormous talents and potential had still hardly become apparent, even to Henslow and Sedgwick. It was during his studies with Sedgwick that Darwin stumbled into a new direction, one that would finally allow him to unlock his hidden potential. The initial key was his reading of *A Personal Narrative of Travels to the Equinoctial Regions of America During the Years 1790–1804* by the most famous scientific explorer of the era, Baron Alexander von Humboldt. The young man became completely fascinated by Humboldt's descriptions of his adventures in the Canary Islands, South America, Mexico, and the United States. At that time much of these lands remained unexplored and unnamed, and sometimes the members of

An eighteenth-century painting of explorer and writer, Alexander von Humboldt.

Humboldt's party were the first Europeans to see them. Darwin longed to be a part of such a voyage of discovery, to break new scientific ground and see such wonders for himself.[11]

To Darwin's surprise and delight, just such a once-in-a-lifetime opportunity soon materialized for him. Henslow wrote to him, saying that the *Beagle*, a vessel piloted by Captain Robert FitzRoy, was about to leave on a five-year trip to explore foreign lands and gather scientific data. FitzRoy needed a naturalist to go on the voyage, and Henslow had personally recommended Darwin for the position. At first the elder Darwin objected, fearing that such an endeavor would delay his son's plans to join the clergy. But these were, after all, really Robert Darwin's plans, not Charles's; and after Josiah Wedgwood wrote a long, impassioned letter on the young man's behalf, Robert relented and gave his consent.

The HMS *Beagle* set sail on December 27, 1831. Darwin shared a tiny cramped cabin with the expedition's surveyor and slept on an uncomfortable hammock that hung above the other man's charts. But the young man was more than willing to suffer such discomforts. He could now say with great pride that he was, officially, what he had long dreamed of becoming—a naturalist; and he kept himself constantly busy. When not collecting and studying plant and animal specimens, he read voraciously and wrote many letters home. Typical was the enthusiasm, maturity, and attention to detail of his May 18, 1832, letter to Henslow, in which he said in part:

> One great source of perplexity to me is an utter ignorance whether I note the right facts, and whether they are of sufficient importance to interest others. . . . On the coast [of South America, near Rio de Janeiro] I collected many marine animals. . . . I took several specimens of an octopus which possessed a most marvelous power of changing colors, equaling any chameleon. . . . Yellowish, green, dark brown, and red, were the prevailing colors. . . . Geology and the invertebrate animals [those without backbones] will be my chief object of pursuit through the whole voyage. . . . I [have] never experienced such intense delight. I formerly admired Humboldt, [and] I now almost adore him; he alone gives any notion of the feelings which are raised in the mind on first entering the tropics.[12]

Ostriches and Tortoise Shells

Though enthusiastic about the possible wonders that lay ahead, Darwin was completely unprepared for the mysterious discoveries

Darwin Records His Observations About Galápagos Animals

In the journal he kept on the Beagle's voyage (excerpted here from The Beagle Record), *Darwin remarks about the fact that many of the species living in the Galápagos Islands strongly resemble, yet remain distinct from, those inhabiting the South American mainland. This observation would later become a major piece of evidence supporting his theory of evolution.*

"I will not here attempt to come to any conclusions, as the species [that I have observed on these islands] have not been accurately examined; but we may infer, that, with the exception of a few wanderers, the organic [living] beings found on this archipelago [island chain] are peculiar to it; and yet that their general form strongly partakes of an American [i.e., South American] character. It would be impossible for anyone accustomed to the birds of Chile and La Plata to be placed on these islands, and not to feel convinced that he was, as far as the organic world was concerned, on American ground. This similarity in type, between distant islands and continents, while the species are distinct, has scarcely been sufficiently noticed [by naturalists and other scientists]. . . . It has been mentioned, that the inhabitants can distinguish the tortoises, according to the islands whence they are brought. I was also informed that many of the islands possess trees and plants which do not occur on the others. . . . Unfortunately, I was not aware of these facts till my collection [of specimens] was nearly completed. It never occurred to me [before this time] that the productions of islands only a few miles apart, and placed under the same physical conditions, would be dissimilar. I therefore did not attempt to make a series of specimens from the separate islands."

about animals that he would make; and he had no inkling that what he would see and learn on this momentous voyage would eventually lead him to write one of the most important books in human history. Among the first of the strange and compelling observations Darwin made on the journey took place in Argentina, in South America. The ship sailed down Argentine rivers, exploring some of the country's inland regions, where Darwin met some gauchos, Argentine cowboys known for their horseback riding skills. They not only invited him to ride with them, but also showed him some rare local animals.

Among these creatures, it was the Argentine ostriches that caught the young naturalist's attention and got him to thinking about the origins of animals. He observed that two distinctly different kinds of ostrich lived in an area encompassing only a few hundred square miles. But how and why should this be?, he asked himself. It made no sense to him that God would create two similar yet still plainly distinct species of ostrich and put them in roughly the same geographic space. At this point in his life, Darwin still accepted the notion that God had created all living things in a few days. In this scenario—part of the religious and social worldview to which the vast majority of Europeans then ascribed—ever since the Creation, plants and animals had maintained the same forms and did not change over time. Darwin did not want to question God's logic. But in the young man's keen sense of reasoning, creating two kinds of ostrich for the same region seemed neither logical nor economical. In the weeks and months that followed, Darwin's instincts told him that some powerful unknown natural principle or force was at work here.

Darwin wondered if he would find other similar examples of strange animal variations as the *Beagle's* voyage continued. In particular, he looked forward to visiting the Galápagos Islands, located along the equator in the Pacific Ocean about five hundred miles off South America's western coast. Because the main Pacific shipping routes did not go anywhere near the small islands in the hundred-mile-long chain, in Darwin's time they remained extremely remote and seldom visited by humans.

Sea lions are among the residents of James Island, in the Galápagos chain.

When the ship finally reached the Galápagos chain in September 1835, Darwin was not disappointed; for it was immediately apparent that these islands were going to live up to their reputation as primitive natural zoos containing creatures that existed no place else on earth. Indeed, finding them inhabited by gigantic tortoises, huge lizards, bright red crabs, and all manner of exotic birds, he felt as though he was witnessing a series of landscapes almost prehistoric in their character.

On the lookout for strange variations in animal species, Darwin found them in abundance in the Galápagos. On one member of the chain, James Island, he and his companions found a colony of giant tortoises that appeared to be deaf, since they did not notice the men until they stepped directly into the creatures' line of sight. Darwin estimated each of the shells of these monstrous beasts to be more than four feet long and about eight feet in circumference. More importantly, the tortoise shells showed him that the same mysterious natural principle that had produced the Argentine ostriches was at work in these Pacific islands. He later studied tortoise shells taken from several different Galápagos Islands and found that slightly different kinds of tortoises lived on different islands. This seemed to confirm what an Englishman on the South American mainland had earlier told him, namely that these shells were so distinct that people on the mainland could easily tell which island a shell had come from.

Darwin's Finches

Even more striking to Darwin were the variations he observed in many of the birds of the Galápagos. He thoroughly enjoyed studying these creatures, of which he counted twenty-six species of land birds

Giant Galápagos tortoises like the ones Darwin encountered when he visited the remote Pacific island chain in the mid-1830s.

A finch feasts on nectar from a cactus flower in Ecuador. In the Galápagos islands, Darwin observed finches that were different from those on the South American mainland.

on James Island and neighboring islands. As in the case of the tortoises, a single species of these local birds often displayed noticeable differences from island to island. For example, the finches on each island had their own uniquely shaped beaks. The finches on one island had thick, strong beaks that they used to crack open nuts and seeds, while the finches inhabiting a neighboring island possessed smaller beaks that were better suited to feeding on fruits and flowers. Another kind of finch featured a beak designed to catch insects, and still another used its beak like that of a woodpecker to extract insect larvae from tree bark.[13]

Why, Darwin wondered, were there so many different types of finch on neighboring islands having the same general climate and terrain? And why were all of these finches similar to, yet still distinctly different from, the finches that lived on the distant South American mainland? Later, in *Origin,* he would write:

> The most striking and important fact [related to the present subject of inquiry] is the affinity of the species which inhabit islands to those of the nearest mainland, without being actually the same. Numerous instances could be given. . . . [But in the Galápagos Islands] almost every product of the land and water bears the unmistakable stamp of the American continent. There are twenty-six land birds; of these twenty-one, or perhaps

21

twenty-three are ranked as distinct species, and would commonly be assumed to have been created [by God]; yet the close affinity of most of these birds to American species is manifest in every character, in their habits, gestures, and tones of voice. So it is with the other animals, and with a large proportion of the plants . . . of this archipelago [island chain]. The naturalist, looking at the inhabitants of these volcanic islands in the Pacific, distant several hundred miles from the continent, feels that he is standing on American land. Why should this be so? Why should the species which are supposed to have been created in the Galápagos . . . and nowhere else, bear so plainly the stamp of affinity to those created in America? There is nothing in the conditions of life, in the geological nature of the islands, in their height or climate, or in the proportions in which the several classes [of animals and plants] are associated together, which closely resembles the conditions of the South American coast. In fact, there is considerable dissimilarity in all these respects. . . . Facts such as these admit of no sort of explanation on the ordinary view of independent creation; whereas on the view here maintained [i.e., the doctrine of evolution], it is obvious that the Galápagos Islands would be likely to receive [animal] colonists from America. . . . Such colonists would be liable to modification, the principle of inheritance still betraying their original birthplace.[14]

Darwin noticed that finches living on the different Galápagos islands were distinct from one another, despite being members of the same species.

By the word "modification," Darwin meant that a species of finch or some other kind of animal seemed to be capable of changing its physical form over time, or put more succinctly—of evolving.

A Compelling and Powerful Idea

By the time Darwin wrote these words, of course, he had had many years in which to think about his observations of the islands, to do further research, and to ponder the greater meaning of it all. Back in the Galápagos, when he was still a young and eager naturalist trying to find his way in the world, he had not yet put two and two together, so to speak. Though he saw and wrote about many strange peculiarities in the plants and animals he encountered during the *Beagle's* voyage, he did not immediately conclude that this was evidence of evolution.

Yet in the weeks, months, and years that followed, such an explanation began to form in his mind, a notion vague and unsupported at first, but relentlessly compelling in its powerful logic, beauty, and simplicity. Perhaps, he came to think, the Galápagos had once been completely barren of life. Over the course of thousands of years, finches from the mainland might from time to time have found themselves caught in wind currents and ended up on the islands. There, they would have found an environment very different from that of the mainland. Many of the plants would have been different, and they would have had to seek out different kinds of foods and adjust to different habits. Eventually, Darwin theorized, after thousands of generations of finches had lived and died, the species would have undergone physical and behavioral change, a tiny bit at a time, in an effort to adjust to its new environment. Furthermore, because the physical conditions differed slightly from island to island, the finches on each island would have adapted in their own various ways and would display slightly different characteristics.

Darwin eventually came to apply the same argument to the tortoises he had encountered in the Galápagos. The first of these creatures, he proposed, might have arrived on the islands after a long sea journey. Over the course of time, the tortoises, like the finches, would have adjusted to their isolated and unique environment by undergoing small, incremental physical changes. In his view, these changes would have allowed the creatures to survive and reproduce better in their strange new surroundings.

As to what actually caused these changes, Darwin was at first stumped. He could think of no logical explanation of how a species could change its form. Yet he could not ignore the vast array of evidence for species undergoing change that he had gathered during the long voyage of the *Beagle*. Thus, even though Darwin did not go so

Lyell's Book Influences Darwin

Just prior to the Beagle's *epic voyage, the ship's captain gave Darwin a copy of the first volume of the great scientist Charles Lyell's* Principles of Geology, *which had a profound influence on the young naturalist. In this excerpt from* Shadows of Forgotten Ancestors, *another great scientist, the late Carl Sagan, explains the crucial themes of Lyell's book.*

"Lyell . . . wrote *Principles of Geology* to advance the 'Uniformitarian' view that the Earth has been shaped by the same gradual processes that we observe today, but operating not merely over a few weeks, or a few thousand years, but ages. There were distinguished geologists who held that floods and other catastrophes might explain the Earth's landforms, but the Noachic [i.e., Noah's] flood wasn't enough. It would take *many* floods, *many* catastrophes. These scientific Catastrophists were comfortable with Lyell's long time scales. But for the biblical literalists [fundamentalists], Lyell posed an awkward problem. If Lyell was right, the rocks were saying that the Bible's six days of Creation, and the age of the Earth deduced by adding up the "begats" [i.e., the succession of human generations mentioned in the book of Genesis], were somehow in error. It was through this apparent hole in Genesis that the *Beagle* would sail into history."

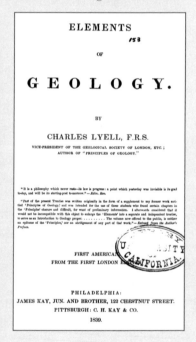

The title page from Lyell's widely influential book, Elements of Geology.

far as to conceive of his theory of evolution while on the trip, he did see and experience many things that channeled his thinking in the direction of evolutionary ideas. He also carefully read and studied the works of some of the great natural scientists of his day, including the masterwork of noted geologist Charles Lyell (whom he would later come to know as a friend). These studies not only opened up new vistas of learning for Darwin, but also helped train him to think like a scientist.

For these reasons, the *Beagle*'s round-the-world journey proved to be the seminal experience of Darwin's career, without which *The Origin of Species* would almost certainly never have come to pass. Many years later, as an old man, Darwin summed up the crucial nature of that experience in shaping his later life and work:

> The voyage of the *Beagle* has been by far the most important event in my life, and has determined my whole career. . . . I have always felt that I owe to the voyage the first real training or education of my mind; I was led to attend closely to several branches of natural history, and thus my powers of observation were improved. . . . I had brought with me the first volume of Lyell's *Principles of Geology*, which I studied attentively; and the book was of the highest service to me in many ways. . . . Everything about which I thought or read was made to bear directly on what I had seen or was likely to see; and this habit of mind was continued during the five years of the voyage. I feel sure that it was this training which has enabled me to do whatever I have done in science.[15]

Darwin's Grand Theory: From Conception to Written Manuscript

More than two decades elapsed between Darwin's return to England in 1836 and his publication of *The Origin of Species* in 1859. During these years he immersed himself in studies of the natural world, drawing partly from his own observations on the voyage of the *Beagle*. He also gathered pertinent information collected by other noted scientists, several of whom he came to know well. In addition, Darwin made numerous new observations of plants and animals and conducted experiments, taking careful notes on everything he learned. From these researches emerged the basic tenets of his theory of evolution, along with an immense amount of evidence to support it. Still, though he became increasingly convinced that he was on the right path, he proceeded slowly, carefully, even painstakingly. It was clear to him that when he did end up publishing his conclusions, he was going to stir up a good deal of controversy. So it was vital to make sure that he had examined, thought through, and then reexamined all the important facts and issues involved; that way he would be better prepared to defend his ideas to the critics he was certain to face.

Darwin's Triumphant Return

At first, however, Darwin did not envision that he would end up writing a major work on the concept of evolution. In fact, during the last weeks of the *Beagle's* voyage, he was still very much in doubt about the future course of his career, not to mention his life in general. He was only twenty-seven, had no job prospects lined up in England, and, as far as he knew, was virtually unknown in the scientific community. Surely, he thought, making a name for himself as a scientist was going to be a slow, difficult process.

In this regard, Darwin was quite mistaken. When the *Beagle* returned to England on October 2, 1836, the young man discovered to his surprise that in his absence he had become a well-known and respected figure in upper-class society and among most scientists as well. To many people, including his proud father and other relatives, therefore, his return was something like that of a triumphant general. This favorable state of affairs was due largely to the diligent efforts of Darwin's former teacher and mentor, John Henslow. The older scientist had frequently sent Darwin's detailed letters describing the voyage and its discoveries to scientists and other scholars; and some of these, and/or commentaries on them, had made their way into various newspapers. The result was that thousands of people had become as fascinated and moved by Darwin's descriptions of unknown lands and creatures as he himself had earlier been by those written by his hero Humboldt.

Fittingly, and also prudently, since it afforded him a way to make needed money, in the next few years Darwin supplied his "fans" with more of the same. After moving into a small London apartment, Darwin wrote a 200,000-word account of his around-the-world voyage and in 1837 published it as *The Journal of Researches into the Geology and Natural History of the Various Countries Visited by H.M.S. "Beagle," Under the Command of Captain FitzRoy, R.N., from 1832 to 1836*. The *Journal* was both a financial and scholarly success for Darwin. On the one hand, from a literary and popular standpoint, it was a worthy successor to Humboldt's *Personal Narrative* and as such captured the imagination of a large reading public. Perhaps more importantly, the *Journal* inspired several younger naturalists to embark on scientific careers of their own. Among them was Joseph Dalton Hooker, who would in time become a world-renowned botanist and one of Darwin's closest friends. The tireless Darwin soon followed up this first volume about exotic lands with others, including *The Structure and Distribution of Coral Reefs* (1842), *Geological Observations on the Volcanic Islands* (1844), and *Geological Observations on South America* (1846).

A nineteenth-century engraving shows the H.M.S. Beagle *passing through the Straits of Magellan at the tip of South America.*

Darwin Expresses Uncertainty About Publication

In a letter to Joseph Hooker, dated May 9, 1856 (quoted here from The Life and Letters of Charles Darwin*), Darwin tosses around the idea of setting down in writing his theory of evolution but cannot seem to decide what form it should take.*

"I very much want advice and *truthful* consolation if you can give it. I had a good talk with Lyell about my species work, and he urges me strongly to publish something. I am fixed against any periodical or journal, as I positively will *not* expose myself to an Editor or a Council, allowing a publication for which they might be abused [by irate critics]. If I publish anything it must be a *very thin* and little volume, giving a sketch of my views and difficulties; but it is dreadfully unphilosophical to give a *resume* without exact references of an unpublished work. But Lyell seemed to think I might do this, at the suggestion of friends, and on the ground . . . that I had been at work for eighteen years, and yet could not publish for several years. . . . Now what think you? I should be really grateful for advice. I thought of giving up a couple of months and writing such a sketch, and trying to keep my judgment open whether or not to publish it when completed. It will be simply impossible for me to give exact references. . . . In the Preface I would state that the work could not be considered strictly scientific, but a mere sketch or outline of a future work in which full references, etc., should be given. Eheu, eheu, I believe I should sneer at anyone else doing this, and my only comfort is, that I *truly* never dreamed of it, till Lyell suggested it. . . . I am in a peck of troubles and do pray forgive me for troubling you. Yours affectionately, C. Darwin."

Attacking the Problem of Transmutation

It was during this period of the late 1830s and early 1840s that Darwin took the initial steps in developing the ideas for what would become his masterwork, *The Origin of Species*. The first of these steps consisted of his increasing obsession with the concept of transmutation. According to this view, plant and animal species are not immutable, or fixed forever in their present forms, but tend to change over time, in the process evolving into new forms. Much of the data Darwin had collected on the *Beagle's* voyage, especially his studies of finches and other creatures off the coast of South America, seemed to show that such evolution was indeed taking place. In and of itself, evolution was far from a new idea. Some ancient Greek scholars had seriously discussed it, as had several eighteenth- and nineteenth-century European scientists, including Darwin's own grandfather Erasmus. What all of Darwin's predecessors in the area had failed to do, however, was to propose a convincing explanation for exactly *how* evolutionary change takes place.

Darwin attacked the problem repeatedly. It seemed to him that nature was somehow "selecting" for survival those species that best adapted to their changing environments and were therefore the most successful. Part of this process, he noted, was observable on a smaller, more controlled scale when humans bred horses, cows, dogs, and other domestic animals. To learn more about the techniques involved, early in 1838 Darwin paid a visit to some English cattlemen who ran large-scale breeding programs. There, he confirmed what he had suspected, namely that the breeders selected the best specimens to sire new generations, thereby increasing the chances of producing strong, successful offspring. They also selected specific cattle having certain desirable characteristics and had these individuals mate, ensuring the reproduction of these characteristics in succeeding generations. For instance, a line of new cows would purposely be bred from older cows that gave a little more milk than an average cow; after several generations, that characteristic would be strengthened

Darwin investigated domesticated cattle like these in an attempt to understand how breeders selected desirable characteristics and passed them on to new generations.

as many of the new offspring would also produce more than the average amount of milk.

The question, of course, was exactly why this technique worked the way it did. Darwin consulted or read the works of experts in the field, and they insisted that such selection of favored animals and traits was an artificial process invented and imposed by humans; it bore no relation, they claimed, to what went on in nature. Yet Darwin suspected that this claim was incorrect, that a similar process *was* at work in nature's far vaster breeding grounds. But though he had arrived at what was basically the right idea, he still had trouble expressing it in clear, logical, and believable terms. "I soon perceived," he later recalled,

> that [nature's] selection [of one species over another] was the keystone of man's success in making useful races of animals and plants. But how selection could be applied to organisms living in a state of nature remained for some time a mystery to me.[16]

When this line of questioning did not lead him to the answers he sought, Darwin decided to approach the problem from a different angle—the process of extinction. If Lyell and those geologists who agreed with him were correct—that geologic and climatic changes occurred gradually over the course of thousands and millions of years—then all natural environments slowly changed as well. That meant that

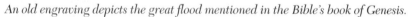

An old engraving depicts the great flood mentioned in the Bible's book of Genesis.

animal species did not always die off suddenly, in huge catastrophes such as Noah's flood (although some might on occasion do so). More often, he reasoned, they became extinct gradually as their environments changed.

Darwin carefully pondered this basic idea for several weeks and suddenly hit on a novel twist. He considered that most other scientists, who accepted the idea of living things being divinely created, based their arguments on the supposition that all animals and plants are perfectly suited to their environments. The prevailing idea was that God would not create living things that were *not* so suited, since this would be contrary to His infallibility and limitless wisdom. But what happens when these environments change over time, Darwin wondered. As the climate and other environmental factors alter an environment, he reasoned, members of a species that had been perfectly suited to the original environment will be less suited to the new one. They will naturally have offspring. Some of these offspring will be like the parents, that is, less suited to the new condition; and these offspring, unable to adapt well, will eventually die off. On the other hand, the offspring of some species will display enough positive physical changes to make them *better* suited to the new environment than their parents had been. Logically, these offspring will tend to survive; moreover, they will produce at least some offspring of their own with similar positive traits, just as in the case of cows that are artificially bred to give more milk.

Darwin, shown here in old age, concluded that animals adapt to changing environments.

Sudden Inspiration from Thomas Malthus

This idea that Darwin had stumbled on was the exact opposite of the process that most other scientists and thinkers assumed to be at work in nature. They held that nature tended to weed out variant (changed) offspring, since in their view any changes would make the species weaker and less able to live in the environment for which it was perfectly suited. Darwin saw that the process actually worked the other way around; nature tended to weed out those offspring that were not variant enough to adapt to the changing conditions of their environment. Still, though this new line of thinking seemed to have the ring of truth, he could not see how it worked on a global scale. How, he wondered, could a few changed, better-off offspring occurring on a random basis account for the worldwide process of evolution that he was sure was taking place? He realized that unless he could deduce the underlying force driving evolution, he would remain in the dark.

Then, on September 28, 1838, like an awesome thunderbolt from on high, a shining ray of light suddenly illuminated Darwin's darkness. He later recalled in his autobiography:

> I happened to read for amusement [the essay by economist Thomas] Malthus on *Population* [which proposes that as human populations grow, more people must compete for the same amount of food], and being well prepared to appreciate the struggle for existence which everywhere goes on from long-continued observation of the habits of animals and plants, it at once struck me that under these circumstances favorable variations would tend to be preserved and unfavorable ones to be destroyed. The result of this would be the formation of a new species.[17]

Tufts University scholar Daniel C. Dennett explains how Darwin applied Malthus's ideas about population growth to his own deductions about natural species undergoing evolutionary change:

> [Malthus] argued that population explosion and famine were inevitable, given the excess fertility of human beings, unless drastic measures were taken. The grim Malthusian vision of the social and political forces that could act to check human overpopulation may have strongly flavored Darwin's thinking. . . . But the idea Darwin [took] from Malthus . . . has nothing at all to do with political ideology, and can be expressed in very abstract and general terms. Suppose a world in which organisms have many offspring. Since the offspring themselves will have many offspring, the population will grow and grow ("geometrically") until inevitably, sooner or later— surprisingly soon in fact—it must grow too large for the available resources (of food, of space [and so on]). . . . At that point . . . not all organisms will have offspring. Many will die childless. . . . Those populations that reproduce at less than the replacement rate are headed for extinction unless they reverse the trend. Populations that maintain a stable population over long periods of time will do so by settling on a rate of overproduction of offspring that is balanced by the vicissitudes [changes] encountered. . . . So the normal state of af-

fairs for any sort of reproducers is one in which more off-spring are produced in any one generation than will in turn reproduce in the next. . . . Darwin added two further logical points to the insight he had found in Malthus. The first was that [in the struggle between competing species] if there was significant variation among the contestants, then any advantage enjoyed by any of the contestants . . . would tip the scales in favor of those who held it. The second was that *if* . . . offspring tended to be more like their parents than like their parents' contemporaries—the biases created by advantages, however small, would become amplified over time, creating trends that could grow indefinitely.[18]

"The Survival of the Fittest"

Darwin was sure that he had discovered the missing piece in the evolutionary puzzle, the piece that had so long eluded him. Just as a group of overpopulated humans would compete with one another to survive, he realized, so too were all living things engaged in a grand contest for survival. In this fierce struggle for existence, he reasoned, all species compete for the same limited supplies of food, water, and territory. Darwin also concluded that the struggle for existence would be most severe among individuals of the same species, for they frequent the same districts, need the same foods, and are faced with the same dangers. Furthermore, and most crucially, nature had evolved a process for weeding out the weaker, less flexible and adaptive varieties and individuals, allowing the stronger, more flexible ones to live on and reproduce. Darwin referred to this process as "natural selection," which he came to see as the driving force behind the process of evolution.

Economist Thomas Malthus, whose essay on population inspired Darwin.

In Darwin's view, survival of individuals within a species or of competing species depends on those individuals and species acquiring and passing on favorable characteristics. Physical characteristics, such as size, strength, shape of body parts, and quality of vision and hearing, regularly pass from parents to offspring. This procedure is random, however, and always results in tiny variations from one generation to another. Following from these facts, Darwin's essential thesis was that nature tends to select, or allow the survival of, those individuals whose variations are favored over those of others; that is, plants and animals that manage to adapt to changing environmental conditions will survive and pass on their favorable characteristics to their offspring. These new, favored kinds of living things will, over time, become increasingly different from their parents, and after the passage of thousands of generations, they will have become so different as to constitute a new species. "If under changing conditions of life," he later wrote in *Origin*,

> organic beings present individual differences in almost every part of their structure . . . if there be, owing to their geometrical rate of increase, a severe struggle for life at some age, season, or year . . . then considering the infinite complexity of the relations of all organic beings to each other and to their conditions of life, causing an infinite diversity in structure, constitution, and habits to be advantageous to them, it would be a most extraordinary fact if no variations had ever occurred useful to each being's own welfare, in the same manner as so many variations have occurred useful to man. But if variations useful to any organic being ever do occur, assuredly individuals thus characterized will have the best chance of being preserved in the struggle for life; and from the strong principle of inheritance, these will tend to produce offspring similarly characterized. This principle of preservation, or the survival of the fittest, I have called Natural Selection.[19]

In this fierce natural struggle resulting in "the survival of the fittest," as he termed it, Darwin further advocated that species with favored characteristics tend to crowd out those that cannot adapt as quickly or as well. These less successful living things inevitably become extinct. Thus, he said, although evolution occurs much too slowly to be directly detectable, its workings can be seen in the fossil record, which reveals the rise and fall of countless species over the eons. Darwin's thesis neatly explained why the most ancient fossils least resemble modern ones. Succeeding generations of offspring become increasingly less like an original set of parents, and the longer evolution proceeds, the less the older forms resemble the new ones.

Amassing the Evidence

It was one thing to conceive such a grand and controversial theory, Darwin realized, and quite another to provide strong and convincing

Down House, where Darwin lived and worked for most of his adult life and also raised his family.

evidence for it. So between 1838 and 1859, which proved to be the two defining decades of his life, he worked on amassing that evidence. During these years he also married his cousin Emma Wedgwood; moved to Down House, a lovely home in the countryside about sixteen miles southeast of London; and began raising a family. He and Emma had ten children in all, but three of these died in infancy.

From the late 1830s on, Darwin was also frequently ill. At first, he assumed that he had caught something ordinary like the flu, but weeks and then months passed, and he only felt worse. In the grip of the mysterious illness, which plagued him nearly the rest of his life, Darwin suffered from headaches, stomach cramps, sleepless nights, and periodic episodes of extreme fatigue. The doctors who examined him over the years could not identify the problem, and none could supply a cure. Modern doctors have tried to diagnose the problem, based on the symptoms described by him and his own physicians. Although it will probably never be confirmed, most modern researchers think that Darwin suffered from Chagas' disease, an infection found mainly in tropical regions. If so, he could easily have contracted the affliction during his fieldwork in South America.[20]

During these same years, Darwin met and became close to Charles Lyell, the renowned geologist whose book he had read while on the *Beagle*. Lyell subsequently introduced Darwin to Joseph Hooker, who supplied Darwin with a great deal of information on plants. Darwin gratefully used this data as he painstakingly continued to piece together the evidence for his theory of evolution. In 1844 Darwin showed Hooker a 230-page outline of the theory. The botanist agreed with many of the conclusions his friend had drawn but still had reservations about the idea of one species actually changing into another; nevertheless, Hooker correctly suspected that Darwin was on to something momentous and urged him to keep working on the project.

Darwin's Priority in Danger?

Encouraged by Lyell and Hooker, as well as by other close associates, including the brilliant biologist Thomas Henry Huxley, in 1856 Darwin began writing a book with the tentative title of *Natural Selection*. Although many years had passed since he had first conceived of his theory of natural selection, the aging naturalist did not want to rush the project. So at first he worked rather leisurely, believing that undue haste would cause him to omit important evidence or arguments. In his mind, to stand up to the scrutiny of the scientific community, the book would have to be meticulously detailed and cover every aspect of the subject. Moreover, he realized, he must attempt to anticipate each of the many opposing arguments that his critics would use against him.

Despite Darwin's insistence on avoiding haste, Lyell and Hooker continued to pressure him to work faster. They reminded him that there was no way to tell who might be working on the same theory; and, if another scientist published it before he did, Darwin would lose his priority—his claim to being the first to publish the theory. (In science, a researcher who registers an invention or publishes an idea before anyone else does is known forever afterward as the originator or discoverer.) Lyell commented that it would be a shame if Darwin lost priority for his unique ideas on evolution after so many years of dedicated work. But Darwin did not share his friend's worry, maintaining that it was highly unlikely that another scientist was working on the very same idea at the same time.

But Darwin was dead wrong. On June 18, 1858, a letter arrived at Down House from Alfred Russel Wallace, a young naturalist who was, at that moment, on an expedition to the East Indies. Wallace, who admired Darwin's writings and had written to the older naturalist a few times before, had enclosed a recently completed essay that he thought Darwin might find interesting. It was titled *On the Tendency of Varieties to Depart Indefinitely from the Original Type.* After quickly reading Wallace's essay, Darwin was both astounded and upset. The younger man had set forth the very same concepts that Darwin had been working on for twenty years; and perhaps even more astonishing, like Darwin, Wallace had found a crucial portion of his inspiration in Malthus's population essay. Unaware of Darwin's work on evolution, the younger naturalist had asked the older one for comments, as well as advice on whether to go ahead and publish the essay. Darwin fully realized that if Wallace did publish it, Darwin's own claim to priority would be lost. Distressed and unsure of what to do, Darwin hastily wrote to Lyell, admitting:

> Your words have come true with a vengeance. . . . I never saw a more striking coincidence; if Wallace had my MS [manuscript] sketch written out in 1842, he could not have made a better short abstract [synopsis]. . . . So all my originality, whatever it may amount to, will be smashed.[21]

Lyell and Hooker acted quickly. They collected Wallace's essay and Darwin's 1944 outline and presented them to the Linnaean Society, a prestigious scientific organization, on July 17, 1858. Hooker testified that he had read Darwin's outline in the mid-1840s, at least a decade before Wallace had even begun to work on his own theory. The Linnaean Society saw to it that both Darwin and Wallace shared credit for the idea but firmly established Darwin's priority. And later Wallace showed the utmost courtesy, publicly acknowledging that Darwin, whom he considered to be a genius, had been the first to develop the theory.[22]

Alfred Russel Wallace, whose own theory of evolution was similar to Darwin's.

Wallace's Theory Remarkably Resembles Darwin's

This is an excerpt from Wallace's essay on evolution (quoted from Just Before Origin: Alfred Russel Wallace's Theory of Evolution*), sent to Darwin in June 1858. Note that the author, unaware of Darwin's work in the same area, had not only arrived at some of the older naturalist's very same conclusions, but also adopted some terminology (such as "struggle for existence") identical to Darwin's own.*

"The life of wild animals is a struggle for existence. The full exertion of all their faculties and all their energies is required to preserve their own existence and provide for that of their infant offspring. The possibility of procuring food during the least favorable seasons, and of escaping the attacks of their most dangerous enemies, are the primary conditions which determine the existence both of individuals and of entire species; and by a careful consideration of all the circumstances we may be enabled to comprehend, and in some degree to explain—the excessive abundance of some species, while others closely allied to them are very rare. . . . Now it is clear that what takes place among the individuals of a species must also occur among the several allied species of a group . . . that those which are best adapted to obtain a regular supply of food, and to defend themselves against the attacks of their enemies and the vicissitudes [changes] of the seasons, must necessarily obtain and preserve a superiority in population; while those species which from some defect of power or organization are the least capable of counteracting the vicissitudes of food, supply, etc., must diminish in numbers, and, in extreme cases, become altogether extinct."

Darwin had learned a valuable lesson from the incident with Wallace. In case there might be other scientists working on evolution, individuals who might pose a threat to his priority, he immediately increased his rate of writing. During the remaining months of 1858 and on into 1859, he worked at what most people would see as a breakneck pace, stopping to rest only when his illness made him too tired to concentrate. The book was finally completed in March 1859, and plans were made for it to be published in November or December of that year as *On the Origin of Species by Means of Natural Selection, or, The Preservation of Favored Races in the Struggle for Life.*

In October Darwin arranged with the publisher (John Murray, who had published Lyell's works) to send some prepublication copies to a number of scientific colleagues, including Lyell, Hooker, Huxley, two old teachers—Henslow and Sedgwick—and Hugh Falconer, a botanist friend. To Falconer, who had been highly critical of some of his work in the past, Darwin enclosed a note that stated in part: "Lord, how savage you will be, if you read it, and how you will long to crucify me alive!"[23] These words turned out to be prophetic. In the months to come, during the public outcry created by the book, a great many people indeed would come to utter the words "Darwin" and "crucify" in the same breath.

CHAPTER 3
Before *Origin:* Pre-Darwinian Theories of Evolution

When Charles Darwin came into the world in 1809, the vast majority of people in European society took it as a given that all of the living things on earth, along with the earth itself of course, had been miraculously created by God. In fact, one of the most common and persuasive arguments for God's existence was known as the "argument from design." It contended that nature and everything within it make up a system so incredibly complex and perfectly interactive that it must have been designed by a being of superior intelligence; and that being could be none other than God. The argument from design was most eloquently stated by eighteenth-century theologian William Paley in his 1802 treatise, *Natural Theology; or, Evidences of the Existence and Attributes of the Deity, Collected from the Appearances of Nature*. Paley uses the now famous analogy of a watch someone finds on the ground. Comparing the workings of the watch to the workings of nature, he states that one must conclude

> that the watch must have had a maker; that there must have existed, at some time and at some place or other, an artificer [maker] or artificers, who formed it for the purpose which we find it actually to answer; who comprehended its construction, and designed its use. . . . Every indication of contrivance, every manifestation of design, which existed in the watch, exists in the works of nature; with the difference, on the side of nature, of being greater or more, and that in a degree which exceeds all computation.[24]

Yet though Paley's view of how living things came to be was the most accepted one, Darwin's ideas about evolution (then commonly called transmutation) did not develop in a vacuum. Indeed, in many ways these ideas were the logical continuation of decades of theory and debate about the age of the earth, the concept of extinction, the meaning of fossils, and the doctrine of evolution itself. Thus, says Peter Bowler,

> Darwin's theory was . . . injected into a culture that was fully aware of what transmutation implied—and Darwin himself was fully aware of the need to accommodate his theory to the preferences of the time. Trying to understand the development and presentation of Darwin's theory without reference

to these earlier debates can only lead to misunderstanding and over-simplification.[25]

Insights from Ancient Greece

Not only was the general theory of evolution not original to Darwin; it was not even original to modern Europe. As in so many other areas of scientific endeavor, the ancient Greeks were the first to suggest that humans and other animals developed from more primitive organisms. The sixth-century B.C. philosopher Anaximenes, for example, proposed that life began growing in ancient slime and over time gave rise to the species known in his day.

Another Greek of that century, Anaximander, advanced some even more extraordinary ideas, among them that the first living creatures came into being in water and that in time these creatures crawled onto the dry land and adapted themselves to their new surroundings. Furthermore, he suggested, human beings developed the same way. "Man came into being from an animal other than himself," said Anaximander, "namely the fish, which in early times he resembled."[26] Though lacking much in the way of evidence and explanation, this theory of organic evolution was the direct, albeit distant, forerunner of the ones developed in Europe in the eighteenth and nineteenth centuries, including Darwin's own.

A later Greek thinker, Empedocles, was impressed by Anaximander's theory of living things and elaborated on it. Empedocles, who lived and worked in the fifth century B.C. in the Greek town of Agrigentum (on the island of Sicily), speculated that at one time many different and varied species had existed. Some of these, he held, were ill-adapted to survive in the harsh conditions of their surroundings, so they died out and stronger, more adaptable species took their place. According to Empedocles:

Empedocles, depicted in this sixteenth-century painting, proposed a theory of evolution.

> Monstrous and misshapen births were created. But all in vain. Nature debarred them from increase [reproduction and survival]. . . . Many species must have died out altogether and failed to

reproduce their kind. Every species that you now see drawing the breath of life has been protected and preserved from the beginning of the world either by cunning or by prowess or by speed.[27]

Astoundingly, without the benefit of the immense wealth of factual data about plants and animals at Darwin's disposal, Empedocles had hit upon the kernel of the idea of natural selection, or "survival of the fittest." Had Empedocles been able to amass such data, he might have further developed the theory and gained a wide following, in which case the history of science would have been very different.

A Young or Ancient Earth?

After the fall of Greco-Roman civilization, for many centuries people no longer questioned or theorized about the origin of life. This was because the Christian Church shaped the thinking of medieval and early modern Europe and perpetuated the view found in the Bible—that God had created the earth and all the animals and plants on it miraculously. An important corollary of this traditional religious view of the Creation was that the earth was very young. In fact, given the information supplied in the Bible, it appeared to be only a few thousand years old. In 1650 a Protestant theologian named James Ussher took the time and effort to examine the generations of the patriarchs, priests, judges, and kings listed in the Old Testament; from his calculations he concluded that the Creation had occurred in 4004 B.C. and Noah's flood in 2349 B.C. A few years later, the noted English scholar John Lightfoot confirmed the bishop's general calculations and issued a slightly refined version. According to Lightfoot, the Creation had taken place at exactly 9:00 A.M. on Sunday, October 23, 4004 B.C.!

Under such time constraints imposed by the religious view of the Creation, there had not been time for species to change little by little and/or become extinct. Therefore very few people even considered such concepts. And those who did felt obligated to make their observations of nature conform to the accepted orthodox view that the world was only about six thousand years old. This did not stop a few from suspecting a much older earth. All around them—in fossils, in sea sediments, in rock layers beneath the ground—scholars increasingly saw evidence that the earth was in fact very ancient. But so strong was religion's hold on society that some scientists ignored this evidence outright.

Other scholars tried to reconcile the geologic evidence with biblical statements and calculations. They suggested that the world was

According to the prominent Protestant theologian James Ussher, the Creation, depicted in this eighteenth-century engraving, took place in 4004 B.C.

indeed much older than Bishop Ussher had decreed, but that God had not revealed this fact in the Bible. According to this view, God had originally created certain species and then destroyed them in Noah's flood. By keeping Noah from preserving these animals on the ark, God had brought about their extinction for His own purposes. This idea of divinely inspired extinction seemed more acceptable, so it became fashionable to identify various unexplained fossils as remnants of creatures from the world before Noah. One common view, for instance, was that a large fossil thighbone discovered in England in 1676 originally belonged to one of a race of giant people mentioned in the Bible.

By the eighteenth century, however, evidence that extinction was a natural phenomenon and that forms of life different from those of the present had once existed was beginning to mount. The first major scientist to champion the idea of natural extinction was French anatomist Baron Georges Cuvier (1769–1832). At an important scientific conference in 1796, he announced his view that large-scale extinctions of animals and plants had occurred frequently in the past. His evidence, with which many other researchers came to agree, implied a much older earth than had been earlier envisioned.

Maupertius's Theory of Evolution

In this changing climate in which science was starting to recognize the reality of a very ancient earth, some scientists began to consider the possibility that other natural forces and processes besides extinction had been at work over the eons. Among these processes was evolution. In this regard, the same intellectual currents that inspired Cuvier influenced one of his countrymen. He was the French scientist-philosopher Pierre Maupertius (1698–1759), who conceived what was, especially for its day, a brilliant theory of the evolution of plants and animals. Like Darwin did later, Maupertius noticed that domestic plant and animal breeders generated new kinds of plants and animals, suggesting that under certain conditions the forms of species were not fixed, but could change.

Moreover, Maupertius attempted to explain how such changes might occur, brilliantly anticipating later discoveries of genes and mutations. As noted scholar Bentley Glass puts it:

> He was . . . the first to apply the laws of probability to the study of heredity. He was led by the facts he had uncovered to de-

Maupertius on Dogs' Toes

In this excerpt from his 1745 work, Venus Physique *(quoted in* Forerunners of Darwin*), Maupertius speculates about the existence of supernumerary (extra) digits in some members of various species, in particular dogs. If, as he suspected, these extra toes were vestiges of once functional structures, it would indicate that the species had undergone physical change over time.*

"There are no animals at all upon whom supernumerary digits appear more frequently than upon dogs. It is a remarkable thing that they ordinarily have one digit less on the hind feet than on those in the front, where they have five. However, it is not at all rare to find dogs who have a fifth digit on the hind feet, although most often detached from the bone and without articulation [joints]. Is this fifth digit of the hind feet then a supernumerary? Or is it, in the regular course, only a digit lost from breed to breed throughout the entire species, and which tends from time to time to reappear? For mutilations can become hereditary just as much as superfluities."

44

velop a theory of heredity that astonishingly forecast the theory of the genes. He believed that heredity must be due to particles derived both from the mother and from the father, that similar particles have an affinity for each other that makes them pair, and that for each such pair either the particle from the mother or the one from the father may dominate over the other, so that a trait may seemingly be inherited from distant ancestors by passing through parents who are unaffected. From an accidental deficiency of certain particles there

Maupertius, the brilliant French thinker who developed an early evolutionary theory.

might arise embryos with certain parts missing, and from an excess of certain particles could come embryos with extra parts, like the six-fingered persons or the giant with an extra lumbar vertebra whom Maupertius studied. There might even be complete alterations of particles—what today we would call "mutations"—and these fortuitous changes might be the beginning of a new species, if acted upon by a survival of the fittest and if geographically isolated so as to prevent their intermingling with the original forms.[28]

Maupertius's "alterations" of the hereditary particles—the mutations—appeared to him to be a primary mechanism in the transmutation of one species into another over time. In his 1751 work, *Nature's System,* he wrote:

Could one not explain by that means [mutations] how from two individuals alone the multiplication of the most dissimilar species could have followed? They could have owed their first origination only to certain fortuitous productions [of offspring], in which the elementary particles failed to retain the order they possessed in the father and mother animals; each

This eastern black shallowtail butterfly has just emerged from its cocoon. Erasmus Darwin pointed out that such creatures undergo major physical transformations.

degree of error would have produced a new species; and by reason of repeated deviations would have arrived at the infinite diversity of animals that we see today; which will perhaps still increase with time, but to which perhaps the passage of centuries will bring only imperceptible increases.[29]

Unfortunately, Maupertius and his truly brilliant ideas were largely rejected and forgotten. This was probably partly because he lacked what Charles Darwin provided later—a mass of observational data collected over several decades to back up the revolutionary tenets of his theory. It would take a great deal of convincing evidence, after all, to mount a successful challenge to the Church and its creationist views.

The Contributions of Erasmus Darwin

The first modern thinker who advocated a well-rounded evolutionary theory, offered some substantial evidence, and was not afraid to stand up to the church was Darwin's grandfather Erasmus (1731–1802). The elder Darwin noted a number of examples of animals undergoing physical change. First, he said, individuals of a species are seen to transform themselves during their life cycles, as in the cases of a caterpillar turning into a butterfly and a tadpole growing into a frog. Second, like both Maupertius and Charles Darwin, he pointed out that certain domestic species of animal—dogs and horses, for example—had long been artificially bred to create new varieties or to enhance favorable characteristics such as strength and speed. Third, Erasmus Darwin called attention to the existence of monstrous births, that is, mutations. He noted that the tendency toward certain mutations seemed to be inherited. "Many of these enormities of shape are propagated," he stated in his *Zoonomia*, "and continued as a variety at least, if not as a new species of animal. I have seen a breed of cats with an additional claw on every foot; of poultry also with an additional claw, and with wings to their feet." These various examples of anatomical change in animals led Erasmus Darwin to conclude that

> they have alike been produced from a similar living filament. In some this filament in its advance to maturity has acquired hands and fingers, with a fine sense of touch, as in mankind. In others it has acquired claws or talons, as in tigers and eagles. In others, toes with an intervening web, or membrane, as in seals and geese.[30]

Having established that animals can and do undergo certain kinds of physical changes, the elder Darwin went a step further and proposed that they evolved over time. This happens, he said, partly because of changes in the creatures' environments and also because of traits they may or may not inherit from their parents. "Would it not be too bold to imagine," he suggested,

> that in the great length of time since the earth began to exist, perhaps millions of ages before the commencement of the history of mankind, would it not be too bold to imagine, that all warm-blooded animals have arisen from one living filament, which The Great First Cause [God's Creation] endued with animality [the state of being an animal] with the power of acquiring new parts, attended with new propensities [tendencies], directed by irritations, sensations, volitions, and associations; and thus possessing the faculty of continuing to improve by its own inherent activity, and of delivering down those improvements by generation to it posterity [descendants], world without end![31]

Although Erasmus Darwin proposed some of the same ideas that his famous grandson did years later, his book and theory did not make the kind of public waves that *The Origin of Species* did. This was partly because the elder Darwin did not present as many detailed explanations and examples as Charles Darwin did. But more importantly, *Zoonomia* appeared at a time when European society was just beginning to recognize the immense age of the earth, as well as the fact that strange animals had once existed and then become extinct;

and not enough educated Europeans were ready yet to consider in a serious way ideas about life's origins that differed from the biblical explanation.

Lamarck's Acquired Characteristics

Nevertheless, Erasmus Darwin's book was widely read among scientists and other thinkers, going through three editions in seven years. And there can be little doubt that his ideas influenced a number of scientists of the next generation who proposed evolutionary concepts of their own. Perhaps the best known and most important of this group was French naturalist Jean-Baptiste Lamarck (1744–1829). His evolutionary theory, usually referred to as transformism, is very similar in a number of ways to that of Erasmus Darwin, leading a number of observers over the years to suspect that Lamarck plagiarized (copied the work of) the older man; however, this charge has never been proven conclusively.

There *is* one major difference between the two theories, namely the choice of a mechanism, or a physical process, that might be causing animal and plant species to evolve over time. Like his grandson, Erasmus Darwin suggested that there is a fierce competition in nature for food and other resources; and the strongest and most adaptable individuals and varieties survive, while the others die out.

The French naturalist Jean-Baptiste Lamarck, whose evolutionary theory was called transformism.

In contrast, Lamarck's proposed evolutionary mechanism involves the inheritance of "acquired characteristics." Bowler explains that this hypothetical process was based on

the assumption that the effects of bodily changes in the adult animal can be passed on to the offspring and can thus accumulate to transform the species. To use one of Lamarck's best-known examples, the efforts made by generations of giraffes trying to reach the leaves of trees are supposed to have gradually lengthened their necks until the modern species was formed.[32]

Couched in modern terms, in order to work in nature, this Lamarckian idea of acquired characteristics would require a situation in which various actions and habits of an adult animal would somehow change the makeup of its genes; and through these changed genes, the animal would pass on small changes in its form or behavior to its offspring. Today, scientists know that this is a completely false assumption. The genes, which carry the genetic code, do not change as a result of what an animal does or experiences in its life. But, of course, Lamarck did not know about

A *model of DNA, the molecule that determines the genetic code of all living things.*

the existence of genes and the blueprint of the genetic code; if he had, he would have rejected outright the notion of acquired characteristics. As it was, quite a number of nineteenth-century scientists, including Charles Darwin himself for a while, either accepted or at least seriously considered Lamarck's idea. And because this idea turned out to be incorrect, in the long run Lamarck's theory of evolution had a negative effect on the progress of evolutionary theory.

It was not so much Lamarck's concept of acquired characteristics, though, that brought him into disrepute in the scientific community. Lamarck also proposed or accepted certain other concepts eventually shown to be false. A conspicuous example was the doctrine of spontaneous generation, which held that living things could spring almost magically from nonliving things (as maggots appeared to spring from rotten meat before people realized that the maggots grow from eggs that flies lay in the meat). Many scientists also came to be critical of Lamarck because they thought that he was an advocate of teleology, the idea that nature has an underlying purpose directed by a greater intelligence. On this point at least, they were wrong; for a careful reading of his works reveals that he was not in fact a teleologist.

Immediate Influences on Darwin?

In the wake of Lamarck, several European scientists speculated about evolution, in a sense preparing the way for Darwin's *Origin.* Between 1810 and 1831, British researchers W. C. Wells (1757–1817), J. C.

Lamarck Advocates an Ancient Earth

One idea that Lamarck got right was the great age of the earth. In these two brief comments, the first from his 1802 work Hydrogéologie, *and the second from an 1805 memoir (both quoted in* Forerunners of Darwin), *he summarizes the importance of this observation. He also points out, to his regret, that most people cannot grasp it and so will not accept much of his work.*

"Oh! how great is the antiquity of the terrestrial globe! and how little the ideas of those who attribute to the globe an existence of six thousand and a few hundred years duration from its origin to the present! The natural philosopher and the geologist see things much differently in this respect; because, if they consider ever so little, first, the nature of fossils spread in such great numbers in all parts of the exposed globe. . . . Second, the number and disposition of the beds, as well as the nature and order of the materials composing the external crust of the globe, studied in a great part of its thickness and in the mass of the mountains, how many occasions they have to be convinced that the antiquity of this same globe is so great that it is absolutely outside the power of man to appreciate it in any manner! . . . These considerations, I know . . . not having obtained the serious examination that I believe they deserve, can only appear extraordinary even to the most enlightened persons. Indeed, man, who judges the greatness of duration only relative to himself and not to nature, will undoubtedly never really find the slow mutations which I have . . . presented and consequently he will believe it necessary to reject without examination my opinion on these great subjects."

Prichard (1786–1848), W. Lawrence (1783–1867), and Patrick Mathew (1790?–1874) attempted to show that Lamarck's theory of acquired characteristics was incorrect. They did not know about the existence of genes either. But their search for a mechanism that drives evolution was at least in the right ballpark, so to speak, for they each proposed ideas that were similar in many respects to "the survival of the fittest" concept that Darwin later developed in tremendous detail. In his 1818 treatise *Essay on Dew,* for instance, Wells discussed the possibility that several different early varieties of humans may have appeared long ago in Africa. Over time, he speculated, one variety would have shown itself to be more able to withstand the local diseases and other environmental factors; as a result, this species would multiply faster than its neighboring cousins and eventually crowd them out in the competition for food and territory. Mathew argued along similar lines, saying that only the hardiest individuals in a given animal population "struggle forward to maturity," while weaker ones die out. "This principle is in constant action," he wrote in his *On Naval Timber and Arboriculture* (1831). "It regulates the color [of the skin], the figure, the capacities and instincts."[33]

It is uncertain if, and in fact unlikely that, Charles Darwin drew any of his inspiration for natural selection from these scientists. They almost certainly got the basic idea from Erasmus Darwin; and Charles Darwin was aware of his grandfather's ideas well before he had ever read their books (if he did indeed read them at all). Still, no scientist works in a vacuum, without a significant amount of influence from his predecessors, and Darwin was no exception. His studies of Humboldt's and Lyell's works constitute only two examples.

Another researcher who influenced Darwin's thinking about evolution was a lecturer whom he had encountered as a young man at the university in Edinburgh—Robert Edmund Grant. All but forgotten now, Grant was an exponent of Lamarckian evolution; and because Lamarck's ideas were generally out of favor in Britain by the 1830s, Grant was not taken very seriously by the scientific community. Darwin obviously did not become an out-and-out Lamarckian as a result of his contact with Grant. But Grant did expose Darwin to a wide range of biological topics with which the younger man had little familiarity and pointed Darwin in the direction of important lines of research. It is an interesting footnote to Darwin's life and work that he later chose to distance himself from Grant. "One day, when we were walking together," Darwin wrote in his autobiography, Grant "burst forth in high admiration of Lamarck and his views on evolution. I listened in silent astonishment, as far as I can judge, without any effect on my mind."[34] Since Darwin held on to some Lamarckian notions for several years before writing *Origin*, it is hard to believe that this last statement is completely accurate and fair.

"Setting the Agenda" for *Origin*

It must be emphasized that, in spite of the speculations of researchers such as Wells, Mathew, and Grant, evolution was not a major topic of public interest or debate in the 1830s and 1840s. It had been a few decades since Lamarck's work had appeared; and the various evolutionary theories mostly circulated among a handful of scientists and other highly educated persons interested in the topic. During the early

1840s, Darwin was working on his own theory of evolution, of course. But he was quietly communicating on a regular basis with Lyell, Hooker, and a few other close colleagues rather than going public.

Then, quite unexpectedly in 1844, a Scottish publisher introduced a book about evolution titled *Vestiges of the Natural History of Creation,* which was similar in some ways to Lamarck's works. The identity of the author was a closely guarded secret for a long time. Only later was it revealed that he was noted Edinburgh publisher and author Robert Chambers, who had a strong interest in evolutionary theories. Evidently Chambers sensed, correctly it turned out, that the educated public was ready to tackle the topic of evolution head-on in a book aimed at laypeople as well as scholars; but he was worried that the storm of protest the book would surely ignite might hurt his livelihood; hence his anonymity.

Vestiges was the last important pre-Darwinian attempt to explain the descent of plant and animal species. And in at least one way it was the most important—namely, it made the general reading public aware of the various ideas and issues related to evolution. As Bowler explains:

> Chambers' purpose was to disassociate evolutionism from its radical image and make it acceptable to the growing middle class. For some years his *Chambers' Edinburgh Journal* had been promoting the message that social progress was inevitable if only people could be given the freedom to innovate. The key to success should be effort and initiative, not aristocratic privilege, and if individuals were given the freedom to exert themselves, society itself would reap the economic and technological benefits. . . . The purpose of *Vestiges* was to argue that social progress is inevitable in the long run because it is a natural extension of the progressive development of life in the course of the earth's history. . . . Chambers [argued] that an ex-

Joseph Dalton Hooker, a great botanist and one of Darwin's closest friends.

Chambers's Book Compared to Lamarck's

Here, from his book Charles Darwin, *the late German scholar Gerhard Wichler explains why, though* Chambers's Vestiges *was similar in many respects to Lamarck's treatise on transformism, Chambers's work was more widely read and discussed than Lamarck's.*

"The two main reasons are, firstly, the clarity with which Chambers arranged his ideas, and secondly the fact that his theories are based to a larger degree on natural science, whilst Lamarck based his work more on natural philosophy. Nowadays, any discussion of the theory of descent is required to give a clear separation of the proofs of evolution, [and] the factors that led to evolution. . . . No such division can be discovered in Lamarck's work; his arrangement is very confused. Chambers, however, carried out this division for the first time. The reader is always grateful for a clear arrangement, especially in a subject as confusing as the problem of the species. . . . [Also] it must be remembered that philosophical trends of thought led Lamarck to believe in the theory of descent. Therefore, a large part of his book was devoted to developing philosophical ideas. Chambers, however, abandoned the belief in the constancy of the species by considering scientific facts, mainly the conception of geological progression. Furthermore, Chambers was able to communicate his own impressions to other people very clearly. Proofs of the theory of descent, as presented by him, became very stimulating and interesting."

pansion of the animal brain in the course of progressive evolution would inevitably lead to the production of the human mind. [He] attempted to soften the blow by arguing that the progressive trend could itself be seen as a continuously operating divine plan of creation. God established the law of development which led to the appearance of successively higher species, instead of creating each new arrival himself.[35]

Though *Vestiges* was thoughtfully written and did an effective job of explaining what evolution was about, it was thinly documented and contained a large number of factual errors. These faults are understandable, considering that Chambers was not a trained scientist. But such errors, along with the author's injection of divine purpose into the mix, made most reputable scientists, including Darwin and Huxley, reject the book. At the same time, the fact that *Vestiges* questioned the literal biblical version of the Creation was enough to condemn it in the eyes of churchmen and conservative thinkers. Despite critical attacks from all quarters, though, Chambers's book accomplished the goal he had set for it—opening a public debate about evolution. "Far from being a failed anticipation of Darwinism," says Bowler, "*Vestiges* established the agenda for all future discussions of evolutionism, including *The Origin of Species*."[36] Indeed, as Darwin witnessed the outcry against *Vestiges*, it was not lost on him that sooner or later he would have to face up to the same court of public opinion. The question was whether he would survive his day in court.

CHAPTER 4

Darwin's Book Receives a Loud and Mixed Reception

The reaction to the publication of *The Origin of Species*, Darwin's massive collection of scientific evidence supporting the theory of evolution, was, as he had expected, loud and mixed. Some scientists and also some educated nonscientists, including a few religious leaders, thought the book fascinating and were willing at least to consider what he had to say. But most people were unwilling to accept any idea or claim that contradicted the biblical explanation for the creation of life. They, like nearly everyone before them, assumed that God had created all species miraculously in a single stroke and that the forms of these plants and animals were immutable. The idea that all of the earth's life-forms have been and remain locked in an eternal, violent struggle in which the strong survive and the weak die out deeply disturbed them; and because they could not see this alleged process of evolution happening before their eyes, they criticized Darwin and rejected his theory.

But despite the numerous assaults on his work and character, some of them quite vicious, Darwin prevailed. This was because the evidence he presented for the workings of the evolutionary process was overwhelming. In page after page, chapter after chapter, he had relentlessly constructed a powerfully convincing case for natural selection. Also, he had fully anticipated the strong objections of many religious people (like himself, for he remained, as he had always been, a believer in God); and in the book's conclusion he appealed to the common sense and fairness of religious leaders and scientists alike, saying:

> I see no good reason why the views given in this volume should shock the religious feelings of anyone. It is satisfactory, as showing how transient [temporary] such impressions are, to remember that the greatest discovery ever made by man, namely, the law of the attraction of gravity [by English scientist Isaac Newton], was also attacked . . . "as subversive of natural, and . . . revealed, religion." A celebrated author . . . has written to me that "he has gradually learnt to see that it is just as noble a conception of the Deity [God] to believe that He created a few original forms capable of self-development into other and needful forms, as to believe that He required a fresh act of creation to supply the voids caused by the action

of His laws." Why, it may be asked, until recently did nearly all the most eminent living naturalists and geologists disbelieve in the mutability [capacity for change] of species? . . . The belief that species were immutable productions was almost unavoidable as long as the history of the world was thought to be of short duration; and now that we have acquired some idea of the lapse of time, we are too apt to assume, without proof, that the geological record is so perfect that it would have afforded us plain evidence of the mutation of species, if they had undergone mutation. But the chief cause of our natural unwillingness to admit that one species has given birth to clear and distinct species, is that we are always slow in admitting great changes of which we do not see the steps. . . . The mind cannot possibly grasp the full meaning of the term of even a million years; it cannot add up and perceive the full effects of many slight variations, accumulated during an almost infinite number of generations. Although I am fully convinced of the truth of the views given in this volume . . . I by no means expect to convince experienced naturalists whose . . . [views are] directly opposite to mine. . . . A few naturalists, endowed with much flexibility of mind, and who have already begun to doubt the immutability of species, may be influenced by this volume; but I look with confidence to the future,—to young and rising naturalists, who will be able to view both sides of the question with impartiality . . . for thus only can the load of prejudice by which this subject is overwhelmed be removed.[37]

Winning Over His Closest Colleagues

With these words Darwin had, in a sense, armed himself for the fight against the "load of prejudice" he knew his book would be up against. But ultimately, he realized, it could well be a generation or two or perhaps even longer before the scientific community as a whole came around to his views. For the moment, he envisioned just one major criteria that would, for him, make the book a success. That would be to win over to his theory his three close friends and scientific compatriots, the great geologist Lyell, the noted botanist Hooker, and the brilliant biologist Huxley. Shortly before *Origin* appeared in print, Darwin wrote to Hooker:

> I remember thinking, about a year ago, that if ever I lived to see Lyell, yourself, and Huxley come round [to an acceptance of the theory of evolution], partly by my book, and partly by their own reflections, I should feel that the subject is safe, and

Biologist Thomas Huxley, one of the most brilliant and outspoken scientists of the nineteenth century, became known as "Darwin's bulldog" for defending his friend.

all the world might rail, but that ultimately the theory of Natural Selection . . . would prevail. Nothing will ever convince me that three such men, with so much diversified knowledge, and so well accustomed to search for truth, could err greatly.[38]

Out of these three men, Darwin knew that Lyell was going to be hardest to convince. But Lyell's acceptance would also be the most decisive and influential in winning over other scientists. This was because by this time he was a sixty-three-year-old living legend and pillar of respect, widely seen as the reigning giant of the physical sciences. There was no question that if Lyell publicly approved of Darwin's thesis, many others, both within and outside of the scientific community, would follow. The problem, as Darwin saw it, was that Lyell was in some ways an old-fashioned, cautious scholar who still hung on to certain traditions, including the orthodox view that God had created animals and plants in some miraculous fashion. True, Lyell had sponsored Darwin's book before the Linnaean Society in 1858 in the incident involving Wallace's essay. But he had done this as a friend and also as a fair-minded scientist who felt that a new theory by a dedicated colleague should receive a fair hearing. It did not mean that he accepted the ideas presented in the book.

For a while, therefore, Lyell sat on the fence, unable or unwilling (or both) to convert publicly to "Darwinism," that is, the doctrine of evolution

The famous geologist Charles Lyell, pictured here, was slow to come around to Darwin's theory.

by natural selection. In 1863, three years after *Origin's* publication, he published a new book of his own, titled *The Antiquity of Man*. Darwin was hopeful that his friend would announce his conversion in that work; however, Lyell still played the skeptic. He seemed to accept that transmutation (evolution) had occurred, but only in the case of animals, suggesting that human beings had somehow been created separately. He also said that even if human transmutation were a fact, it did not necessarily rule out a designer (God). "I think the old 'creation' is almost as much required as ever," he wrote to Darwin. "But you ought to be satisfied, as I shall bring hundreds [of scientists and other educated people] towards you, who if I treated the matter more dogmatically, would have rebelled."[39] Eventually, though, Lyell could no longer resist the comprehensiveness and intellectual power of Darwin's views and evidence. In the tenth edition of his *Principles of Geology*, published in 1867, Lyell finally announced his conversion to the mutability of species, largely as explained in Darwin's *Origin*.

Hooker's and Huxley's conversions to Darwinism came much quicker and easier than Lyell's. As City University of New York scholar Gertrude Himmelfarb tells it, when Hooker

> publicly announced his adherence [to Darwin's theory], at the meeting of the British Association in 1860, he described himself as one who had been apprised of [shown] the theory fifteen years earlier, had vigorously argued against it . . . and had only been persuaded of its truth when facts otherwise inexplicable became intelligible as a result of it. Thus, as he described it, conviction was "forced upon an unwilling convert." It is the unwilling convert who makes the most effective witness in a cause and is likely to be its most enthusiastic communicant. The eyes of the world and of posterity were upon science, Hooker

warned one lagging colleague. . . . "Above all things," he counseled, "remember that this reception of Darwin's book is the exact parallel of the reception that every great progressive move in science has met with in all ages" . . . [and therefore] progressive scientists had the duty of supporting it.[40]

As for Huxley, perhaps the most fearless and outspoken scientist of the day, almost immediately after *Origin*'s debut he appointed himself Darwin's chief defender. In fact, he soon became known as "Darwin's bulldog" for his loud and relentless support of his friend's theory. "My reflection," Huxley later wrote,

> when I first made myself master of the central idea of the *Origin* was, "How extremely stupid not to have thought of that!" . . . Darwin and Wallace dispelled the darkness [surrounding the subject of life's origins], and the beacon-fire of the *Origin* guided the benighted. . . . The only rational course for those who had no other object than the attainment of truth was to accept "Darwinism" as a working hypothesis and see what could be made of it. Either it would prove its capacity to elucidate the facts of organic life, or it would break down under the strain. This was surely the dictate of common sense, and, for once, common sense carried the day.[41]

Converts and Critics

Indeed, common sense did seem to prevail, at least among scientists, in the first few years following *Origin*'s publication in December 1859. Darwin had stated in the book that no false theory could possibly explain so much so well. And one scientist after another seemed to agree, for the more they thought about what he had written and applied his views to the observable world, the stronger his case looked. According to scholar Tom McGowen:

> It is a common happening in science that any theory based on incorrectly understood evidence or faulty reasoning eventually gets demolished by the work of other scientists, whereas a theory based fully on fact gains strength as new evidence comes to light, as was the case with [Polish astronomer Nicolaus] Copernicus' theory that the earth revolved around the sun. And even as the arguments about evolution were going on, new evidence was accumulating to back up Darwin's theory. . . . The discovery in 1856 of fossil skeletons of an apparently different human species [the Neanderthals] . . . showed that there had indeed been a more primitive kind of human.

Huxley's Conversion to Darwinism

This tract by Darwin's friend, Thomas Henry Huxley (quoted from Leonard Huxley's collection of T. H. Huxley's letters) recalls in part how the great biologist became a convert to the theory of evolution as explained by Darwin.

"I imagine that most of those of my contemporaries who thought seriously about the matter, were very much in my own state of mind—inclined to say to both [creationists] and evolutionists, 'a plague on both your houses!' [a line spoken by the character Mercutio in Shakespeare's *Romeo and Juliet*] and disposed to turn aside from an interminable [very lengthy] and apparently fruitless discussion, to labor in the fertile fields of ascertainable fact. And I may therefore suppose that the publication of the Darwin and Wallace paper in 1858, and still more that of the *Origin* in 1859, had the effect on them of the flash of light which, to a man who has lost himself on a dark night, suddenly reveals a road which, whether it takes him straight home or not, certainly goes his way. . . . The *Origin* provided us with the working hypothesis [about life's origins] we sought. Moreover, it did the immense service of freeing us forever from the dilemma—Refuse to accept the creation hypothesis, and what have you to propose that can be accepted [in its place] by any cautious reasoner? In 1857 I had no answer ready, and I do not think that anyone else had. A year later we reproached ourselves. . . . My reflection when I first made myself master of the central idea of the *Origin* was, "How extremely stupid not to have thought of that!" . . . Darwin and Wallace dispelled the darkness [surrounding the subject of life's origins], and the beacon-fire of the *Origin* guided the benighted."

And the discovery of the fossil remains of a prehistoric creature that was clearly a combination of both reptile and bird [the *Archaeopteryx*] . . . was a titanic piece of proof for Darwin's claim that birds had evolved from reptiles.[42]

In fact, Darwin's book seemed to explain so much, so well about plants and animals that many of the world's most renowned scientists joined the ranks with Hooker, Huxley, and eventually Lyell in praising it. Many of the favorable reviews of the volume echoed the one written by Hooker for the December 31, 1859, issue of the *Gar-*

dener's Chronicle. "We have risen from the perusal [examination] of Mr. Darwin's book," he stated,

> much impressed with its importance. . . . It is a book teeming with deep thoughts on numberless simple and complex phenomena of life; its premises in almost all cases appear to be correct; its reasoning is apparently close and sound, its style clear, and we need hardly add its subject and manner equally attractive and agreeable; it is also a perfectly ingenuous book, bold in expressions as in thought where the author adduces what he considers clear evidence. . . . Whatever may be thought of Mr. Darwin's ultimate conclusions, it cannot be denied that it would be difficult in the whole range of the literature of science to find a book so exclusively devoted to the development of theoretical inquiries, which at the same time is throughout so full of conscientious care, so fair in argument, and so considerate in tone.[43]

Subsequently, as the book sold out in printing after printing, increasing numbers of scholars and other educated people found Darwin's arguments just as compelling and inescapable as Hooker did. So powerful were these arguments, that by the end of the 1860s nearly every important scientist in the world had accepted either some or all of them. As early as 1863, Darwin's friend the Reverend Charles Kingsley wrote to a colleague, "Darwin is conquering everywhere and rushing in like a flood, by the mere force of truth and fact."[44]

The skull of a Neanderthal (right) and a possible reconstruction of its face. Discoveries of Neanderthal remains confirmed that earlier forms of humans had once existed.

Still, certainly some scientists and other thinkers were not so impressed with Darwin's ideas. These more conservative individuals tended, as Lyell had for a while, to stick by and defend the traditional creationist version of life's origins; and they worried that the acceptance of Darwinism by so many of their colleagues might pervert and degrade both science and society by putting humans on a par with beasts.

Fairly typical of the negative reviews of *Origin* after its release was that written by Darwin's old teacher Adam Sedgwick for the April 7, 1860 issue of the widely read *Spectator.* Sedgwick admitted that Darwin was right to point out that varieties of dogs and other domesticated animals can and do undergo change. However, these changes were the result of "human design." God would not allow such change to happen in nature, said Sedgwick, where "wild animals of different species do not desire to cross and unite." Further, "species have remained constant for thousands of years; and time . . . though multiplied by millions and billions [of years], would never change them, so

Darwin's Theory a "String of Air-Bubbles"?

This is part of scientist Adam Sedgwick's unfavorable review of Darwin's The Origin of Species *(taken from the April 7, 1860, issue of the* Spectator*).*
I must in the first place observe that Darwin's theory is not *inductive*, not based on a series of acknowledged facts that point to a *general conclusion,* not a proposition evolved out of the facts, logically, and of course including them. . . . The pretended physical philosophy of modern days strips Man of all his moral attributes, or holds them of no account in the estimate of his origin and place in the created world. A cold atheistical materialism is the tendency of the so-called material philosophy of the present day. Not that I believe that Darwin is an atheist; though I cannot but regard his materialism as atheistical; because it ignores all rational conception of a final cause. I think it untrue because [it is] opposed to the obvious course of Nature. . . . I therefore think it intensely mischievous. Let no one say that it is held together by a cumulative argument. Each series of facts is laced together by a series of assumptions, which are mere repetitions of the one false principle. You cannot make a good rope out of a string of air-bubbles."

The imposing front courtyard of Britain's prestigious Oxford University. It was here in 1860 that Huxley and Hooker faced down Darwin's enemies and won the day.

long as the conditions remained constant." If the conditions did change, new species might appear, but only through the handiwork of God. "For I can see in all [the natural wonders] around me a design and purpose . . . which prove that there is exterior to, and above, the mere phenomena of Nature a great prescient and designing cause." Sedgwick also complained that Darwin's theory was too materialistic; that is, it seemed to reduce the nobility of human intelligence and morality to mechanical and bestial principles, thereby going against God's intentions. "By gazing only on material nature," the review went on, "a man may easily have his very senses bewildered. . . . He may become so frozen up, by a too long continued and exclusively material study, as to lose his relish for moral truth."[45]

The Great Oxford Debate

Seen in retrospect, the whole battle between Darwin's supporters and critics can be glimpsed in miniature in a single dramatic episode, now one of the most famous in the annals of science. In June 1860, only some six months after the publication of *Origin,* a meeting of the British Association for the Advancement of Science was scheduled to be held at the prestigious Oxford University. Darwin was not looking forward to the gathering, for it was rumored that his major opponents were planning to attend and strike a death blow at the "offensive" book and its author. The creationists had chosen as their champion the highly respected bishop of Oxford, Samuel Wilberforce. Because the bishop knew little about science, a leading anti-Darwinian scientist, Richard Owen (best known for coining the word "dinosaur"), carefully

Samuel Wilberforce, the bishop who attempted to blacken Darwin's name.

coached Wilberforce, supplying him with arguments to use against Darwin. Meanwhile, knowing that Darwin's illness made him too weak to attend the meeting, Huxley and Hooker prepared to do battle in their friend's stead.

On June 28, 1860, more than seven hundred people crowded into the university's library, many of them hoping to see *Origin*'s ideas smashed and its author discredited. Wilberforce spoke first. Following Owen's instructions as best as he could, he attempted to make light of Darwin's ideas, asking early on if anyone in the audience had ever actually seen animals and plants evolving. Of course they had not, Wilberforce proclaimed, for these species were the same today as they were when God made them. The bishop then asked, in a scoffing tone, whether any kinds of turnip might someday evolve into human beings, a deliberate attempt to distort Darwin's views (since Darwin never suggested that plants evolved into animals). For a long time, Wilberforce continued to denounce Darwin and even went so far as to attack Huxley, who was sitting nearby. Finally, the bishop turned to Huxley and rudely asked whether it was through his grandfather or grandmother that he claimed descent from apes.

As Wilberforce received a loud round of applause and took his seat, Huxley stood and walked to the lectern. Briefly, easily, and firmly, he rebutted each of the bishop's attacks, adding that his opponent did not even appear to understand the ideas he was denouncing. Then Huxley addressed Wilberforce's uncalled-for remark about his ancestry. "A man has no reason to be ashamed of having an ape for his grandfather," the great scientist asserted.

> If there were an ancestor whom I should feel shame in recalling, it would be a *man*, a man of restless and versatile intellect, who, not content with . . . success in his own sphere of activity, plunges into scientific questions with which he has no real acquaintance, only to obscure them by an aimless rhetoric, and distract the attention of his hearers from the real point at issue by eloquent digressions, and skilled appeals to religious prejudice.[46]

As Huxley affirmed his preference for an ape over a man like Wilberforce, the crowd went wild, with Darwin's opponents and supporters shouting at the speakers and at one another as well. Seeing how a supposed scientific meeting had degenerated into mob rule, the mild-mannered Hooker became both angry and disgusted. When the commotion finally died down, he rose and strode with a commanding and purposeful gate to the lectern. The audience now sat in stunned silence as the foremost botanist in the world demolished Wilberforce's arguments one by one. For more than two hours, Hooker lectured with passion and conviction, explaining Darwin's views without distortion or ridicule. And when he finally sat down, to everyone's surprise, it was Wilberforce and Owen, not Darwin, who had been discredited.

Following Up on *Origin*

Though thoroughly embarrassed, however, Darwin's opponents had not been defeated in the Oxford debate. They continued to be vocal during his final years and would remain so in the century that followed his death. Yet they could not erase the very real and permanent effects of the publication of *The Origin of Species*. The book had not only changed the course of science forever, but also significantly altered the life of its author. Whether one accepted Darwin's ideas or not, considered him harmless or dangerous, loved him or hated him, there was no denying that he was now a world-renowned figure. Important public people and newspapers regularly discussed, quoted, defended, or criticized him; and for the rest of his days, a long line of distinguished scientists, theologians, and other scholars made pilgrimages to Down House in Kent. This was the only way they could meet and converse with him in person, for he had become almost literally a recluse. In large part because of his continued ill health, but also because he was shy and retiring by nature, he left Huxley and others to travel the world defending his ideas and rarely ventured from the peaceful and secure atmosphere of his home.

An aged and contemplative Charles Darwin sits outside Down House.

Moreover, he became thin, bald, and grew a long white beard, all of which made him appear much older than he actually was.

Yet Darwin still remained busy, sometimes puttering in the garden, other times conducting new plant experiments, and year after year managing to maintain an impressive output of books and articles. In 1867, for instance, he began work on *The Descent of Man*, the natural follow-up to *Origin*. Ironically, much of the fuss attending the publication of *Origin*, including some of Wilberforce's remarks at Oxford, had been based on Darwin's supposed suggestion that human beings had descended from beasts, which to many people seemed degrading. Yet the reality was that *Origin* had not dealt directly with human evolution. It had instead focused most of its attention on natural selection and other natural processes, presenting facts about plants and animals as evidence.

In *Descent*, published in 1871, Darwin finally plunged headlong into the subject of human evolution, his main purpose being to show that it was possible for an organ as complex as the human brain to evolve via natural selection. He did not suggest, as is still commonly assumed by those who have not actually read his works, that humans had descended from apes. In his view, both apes and humans had evolved from some common, less-complex ancestor.

Darwin had anticipated that *Descent*'s publication would elicit some of the same cries of outrage that had greeted *Origin*. But much to his surprise, the storm of protest he had expected never materialized. There were a few unkind jabs at his character and the usual journalistic lampoons, to be sure. The English magazine *Hornet*, for example, printed a cartoon showing his bearded head atop a gorilla's torso. But for the most part, critical reviews were tame. The outspoken Huxley commented that the "mixture of ignorance and insolence" that had characterized many of the reviews of *Origin* were "no longer the sad distinction of anti-Darwinian criticism."[47]

The Power of Genius and Truth

As it was, Darwin never again had to worry about negative public reactions to his works. This was mainly because his later treatises were very scholarly tracts about insects, worms, plants, and so on, and of limited interest to all save a handful of biologists, botanists, and horticulturists. While working on these volumes, Darwin remained always at Down House, leaving its walls only to take walks through the nearby fields. He was often accompanied by visitors, for the pilgrimages of his fans continued unabated. One young researcher was so anxious about meeting his hero that when he finally did so he found himself physically unable to speak and finally burst into tears. The modest and unassuming Darwin never ceased to be mystified by such adoration.

Darwin was equally mystified when, in the late 1870s, the strange, unidentified illness that had plagued him for three decades suddenly and inexplicably disappeared. Unfortunately, though, his by now frail body had already sustained too much damage to allow a restoration of his health. In December 1881 and again a few months later, he suffered heart seizures; and on April 19, 1882, he died at the age of seventy-three at Down House. A week later, in a solemn ceremony, his coffin

The magnificent Westminster Abbey, where Darwin was laid to his final rest.

was carried into London's Westminster Abbey and placed near the final resting place of his own hero, Isaac Newton, another man whose ideas had changed the world. The faithful Huxley further linked these two giants of science in the following words, which can stand as a fitting epitaph to Darwin and his masterwork, *The Origin of Species.*

> The name of Charles Darwin stands alongside [that] of Isaac Newton . . . [and] calls up the grand ideal of a searcher after truth and interpreter of Nature. . . . [He was] a rare combination of genius, industry, and unswerving veracity [truthfulness], who earned his place among the most famous men of the age by sheer native power. . . . And with respect to that theory of the origin of forms of life . . . with which Darwin's name is bound up as closely as that of Newton with the theory of gravitation . . . "the struggle for existence" and "natural selection" have become household words and everyday conceptions. . . . No one doubts their vast and far-reaching significance. Wherever the biological sciences are studied, *The Origin of Species* lights the paths of the investigator; wherever they are taught, it permeates the course of instruction.[48]

CHAPTER 5 Modern Acceptance and Rejection of Darwinian Evolution

The truly enormous impact of Charles Darwin's *Origin of Species* in the past century or so has been twofold. On the one hand, and most importantly, most of the ideas expounded in the book have stood the test of time and remained crucial guideposts for modern researchers in the biological sciences. "The basic theory of evolution has been confirmed so completely that modern biologists consider evolution simply a fact," says world-renowned zoologist Ernst Mayr.

How else except by the word "evolution" can we designate the sequence of faunas [animals] and floras [plants] in precisely dated geological strata? . . . It is as much a fact as the observation that the earth revolves around the sun rather than the reverse. . . . The greatest triumph of Darwinism is that the theory of natural selection . . . is now the prevailing explanation of evolutionary change. It has achieved this position both by irrefutable proofs and by default, as all the opposing theories were demolished. . . . One hundred and thirty years of unsuccessful refutations [by Darwin's opponents] has resulted in an immense strengthening of Darwinism.[49]

On the other hand, those who have remained unwilling to accept the doctrine of evolution in general, and Darwin's version as presented in *Origin* in particular, have carried on their fight against it. Creationists, who are typically nonscientists, continue to insist that Darwin's theory is *not* a fact and that it does not refute the biblical explanation of the origins of life. Their modern movement, based mainly in the United States, sees the teaching of evolution in schools as a threat to traditional Christian beliefs; many creationists fear that learning about evolution might confuse, twist, and corrupt their children's minds and cause them to turn away from religion and its moral teachings. Consequently, they have mounted one attempt after another either to ban teaching of evolution or to allow the biblical version to be given equal time in the classroom. Thus, though accepted with little reservation by the scientific community, Darwinian evolution remains nearly as controversial today as when *Origin* appeared in 1859.

Religious Modernism Versus Religious Fundamentalism

Ironically, even religious leaders did not originally foresee this turn of events. In the decades that immediately followed the book's publication, a good many theologians and other religious thinkers came to accept Darwin's ideas about evolution, either fully or in part. This was due in some degree to the directions biblical scholarship was taking at the time. A number of respected nineteenth-century biblical scholars mounted

Tenets of Creationist Doctrine

These are some of the basic articles of faith listed by the Institute for Creation Research, in Santee, California.

"—The physical universe of space, time, matter, and energy has not always existed, but was supernaturally created by a transcendent personal Creator who alone has existed from eternity.

—The phenomenon of biological life did not develop by the natural processes from inanimate systems but was specially and supernaturally created by the Creator.

—Each of the major kinds of plants and animals was created fundamentally complete from the beginning and did not evolve from some other kind of organism. . . .

—The first human beings did not evolve from an animal ancestry, but were specially created in fully human form from the start. . . .

—The record of earth history, as preserved in the earth's crust, especially in the rocks and fossil deposits, is primarily a record of catastrophic intensities of natural processes, operating largely within uniform natural laws, rather than one of gradualism and relatively uniform process rates. . . .

—The universe and life have somehow been impaired since the completion of creation, so that imperfections in structure, disease, aging, extinctions, and other such phenomena are the result of "negative" changes in properties and processes occurring in an originally-perfect created order."

detailed studies of early versions of the Bible, as well as the cultures of the peoples who lived in the ancient lands described in that book. These researchers made it clear that the Old Testament had been produced over a span of several hundred years by a variety of authors. Moreover, many biblical stories had been based on or influenced by the legends of ancient Middle Eastern peoples such as the Babylonians, suggesting that at least some of the Bible had to be regarded as fable or allegory. As a result, numerous religious leaders tried to reconcile the Bible with new and widely accepted scientific discoveries; for example, one increasingly popular view was that evolution was God's grand design for a kind of "ongoing" creation. This merging of religious and scientific ideas became known as "religious modernism."

Socially and educationally speaking, the combined effects of religious modernism and the scientific community's general acceptance of the main tenets of *The Origin of Species* were significant. By 1900, four decades after the book's publication, the great controversy it had ignited had largely died down. Most biology textbooks now routinely included sections on evolution and those that did not rapidly became outdated. This trend continued and accelerated until, by 1920, nearly every college and high school in both Europe and the United States taught evolution in biology classes.

But as it turned out, to the surprise of most scientists and teachers, the controversy about evolution and religion was far from over. All through the late 1800s and early 1900s, the fundamentalists, primarily Americans who lived in the rural South (the so-called "Bible belt"), remained outside of the intellectual mainstream of the major organized religions by refusing to accept Darwin's ideas. They got their name from a series of ten pamphlets, titled *The Fundamentals*, that appeared in 1910. These writings, which circulated throughout the United States in the following years, were a reaction by very conservative biblical literalists to what they saw as a steady erosion of traditional faith in the Bible in favor of "godless" science. *The Fundamentals* tried to redefine what it meant to be a Christian, stressing the "Five Points" of true belief. These were the complete infallibility of the Bible; the virgin birth of Jesus Christ; Christ's voluntary death to atone for humanity's sins; Christ's resurrection into Heaven; and the authenticity of all miracles described in the Bible.

This conservative and rigid religious doctrine appealed to a growing number of people, and the fundamentalist movement rapidly gained steam in the United States and Canada. At first, small fundamentalist factions grew within established religious denominations such as the Methodists and Baptists; later, after an interdenominational fundamentalist meeting—the World Bible Conference—was

In the early twentieth century, a number of American Christians became fundamentalists, who advocate that Christ's resurrection after his crucifixion is a fact.

well attended in Philadelphia in 1919, Dr. William Bell Riley, a Minnesota minister, helped found the World Christian Fundamentals Association. By the early 1920s, fundamentalism had gained a major voice in American religion.

The Destruction of Children's Faith?

Within that collective voice, the outstanding *individual* voice was William Jennings Bryan (often called the "Great Commoner"), for over thirty years one of the leading politicians and far and away *the* leading religious speaker in the United States. Interestingly, though a biblical literalist throughout his life, he had not always been an anti-evolutionist; as a young man, while he did not accept the theory of evolution, neither did he condemn it or its appearance in school curricula. Later, however, he learned the results of some informal polls that suggested that over half of the scientists in the United States doubted or denied the existence of God and that nearly half of graduating college students also expressed a lack of faith. This deeply disturbed Bryan, who came to the conclusion that such loss of faith was directly proportional to the acceptance of evolutionist theory. And he began to denounce evolution in his

William Jennings Bryan, the "Great Commoner." In 1925, he led the prosecution team in the now famous Scopes trial, which took place in Dayton, Tennessee.

speeches. "Survival of the fittest," he warned, might bring about "a life-and-death struggle from which sympathy and the spirit of brotherhood are eliminated. It is transforming the industrial world into a slaughter-house."[50]

Thanks to Bryan and influential religious leaders who sympathized with his views, opposing the "dangerous" doctrine of evolution became a zealous and defining cause of the fundamentalist movement. By the early 1920s, all fundamentalists had come to agree that the most dangerous aspect of Darwin's theory was its "intrusion" into public school curricula, where it threatened to destroy the faith of a whole generation of children. This perceived threat against religious faith was the motivating factor behind the fundamentalist crusade to drive the teaching of evolution out of the schools.

The crusade's initial legal battles were unsuccessful. Among these were the attachment of an anti-evolution clause to a financial bill in the South Carolina legislature in 1921; a 1922 Kentucky bill that would have banned the teaching of "Darwinism, atheism . . . and evolution insofar as it pertains to the origin of man"; in the same year another South Carolina bill, this one designed to withhold money from schools that taught "the cult known as Darwinism"; and similar anti-evolution bills in Florida and Texas.[51]

Although for various reasons these particular bills never became law, the fundamentalists did manage to score some modest victories. In 1923, for example, Oklahoma passed a bill that banned textbooks containing descriptions of evolution (though the actual teaching of evolution remained legal); and in North Carolina in 1924, despite the defeat of an anti-evolution bill in the state legislature, fearful school officials removed biology textbooks featuring chapters on evolution from all of the state's high schools.

The World-Famous Scopes Trial

What seemed to be the fundamentalists' first *major* success came in 1925, when a Tennessee state legislator named John Washington Butler,

Tennessee's Butler Act

This is the complete text of the controversial Butler Act (quoted in Ginger's Six Days or Forever?*), which the Tennessee legislature passed in March 1925, igniting the controversy that led to the Scopes trial.*

"An Act prohibiting the teaching of the Evolution Theory in all the Universities, Normals, and other public schools of Tennessee, which are supported in whole or in part by the public school funds of the State, and to provide penalties for the violations thereof.

Section 1. Be it enacted by the General Assembly of the State of Tennessee, That it shall be unlawful for any teacher in any of the Universities, Normals and other public schools of the State which are supported in whole or in part by the public school funds of the State, to teach any theory that denies the story of the Divine Creation of man taught in the Bible, and to teach instead that man has descended from a lower order of animals.

Section 2. Be it further enacted, That any teacher found guilty of the violation of this Act shall be guilty of a misdemeanor and upon conviction, shall be fined not less than One Hundred ($100.00) Dollars nor more than Five Hundred ($500.00) Dollars for each offense.

Section 3. Be it further enacted, That this Act take effect from and after its passage, the public welfare requiring it."

a former rural farmer, introduced his own anti-evolution bill. The Butler Act, which prohibited the teaching of evolution and provided for penalties of from $100 to $500 for violators, passed the Tennessee legislature on March 13, 1925. The state's governor, Austin Peay, a deeply religious man himself, signed the Butler Act into law on March 21, giving this justification: "It will not put our teachers in any jeopardy. Probably the law will never be applied. . . . Nobody believes that it is going to be an active statute."[52]

But Governor Peay was wrong in his assumption that the law would never be applied. On May 7, 1925, about six weeks after the passage of the Butler Act, John Scopes, a high school science teacher in Dayton, Tennessee, was arrested for breaking the new law. The arrest and the world-famous trial that grew out of it were part of an orchestrated plot by prominent local citizens and officials, Scopes himself among them. Some of these men thought the Butler Act was unfair, unnecessary, and educationally backward, while others held that the law might be a good thing. Out of their spirited discussion of the matter emerged their primary goal—to test whether the new law was constitutional. (The Dayton "conspirators" also unanimously agreed that such a test case would attract attention to their tiny, out-of-the-way town and maybe help drum up some extra business.)

The great trial lawyer Clarence Darrow (standing with his arm upraised) makes a point to the jury in the packed courtroom during the Scopes Trial.

The Scopes trial took place from July 10 to 21, 1925, in Dayton and attracted huge crowds and global press coverage. The leading prosecutor was none other than the Great Commoner himself, William Jennings Bryan; while the defense (supported by the American Civil Liberties Union, or ACLU) managed to secure the services of the most famous trial lawyer of the early twentieth century, Clarence Darrow. Although Darrow promised to bury the prosecution under a mountain of scientific testimony, the judge did not allow any discussion of Darwin's theory of evolution. The only relevant question, the judge insisted, was whether Scopes had violated the Butler Act. Since the defense openly admitted that the teacher had indeed broken the law, it appeared to be an open-and-shut case.

On July 20, however, Darrow shrewdly managed to get Bryan to take the stand as an expert witness on the Bible. During the long, dramatic verbal duel between these two giants, Darrow led his opponent, who possessed almost no scientific knowledge, into confusion and thoroughly embarrassed him. The result was that, though the jury found Scopes guilty and the judge fined him $100, public opinion perceived that the defense had won an intellectual and moral victory. Ironically, the Tennessee Supreme Court later overruled Scopes's conviction on a technicality; and evolution continued to be taught in Tennessee's schools, despite the fact that the Butler Act was not repealed until 1967.

The Anti-Darwinian Forces Continue Their Fight

In the years following the Scopes trial, the creationists continued their fight against the "dangerous" ideas of Darwin's *Origin of the Species*. A law similar to the Butler Act passed in Mississippi in 1926; however, that same year the Kentucky and Louisiana legislatures rejected anti-evolution bills. Meanwhile, the press, as well as scientists and academic spokespersons across the nation, continued to depict those who advocated such laws as backward and ignorant. The immediate result was that the fundamentalist drive to censor science in the schools steadily lost steam.

But this situation proved to be only temporary, for the creationists eventually found a new, more promising approach to promoting their views. By the late 1960s, laws like the Butler Act had been ruled unconstitutional and there was no way to teach the Bible in public schools because that violated the First Amendment's clause about separation of church and state. To get around these obstacles, beginning in the 1970s the creationists lobbied for "equal time" and "balanced treatment" in classrooms, arguing that evolution was only "one of the theories" for human origins. The biblical creation was another and equally worthy theory, they insisted, and should therefore be taught right alongside evolution in biology classes. These efforts were unsuccessful until 1981, when a bill, titled Act 590, came before the Arkansas legislature. Act 590 provided that if human origins were discussed in a public classroom, the teacher must cover "Creation-science" along with "Evolution-science."

Immediately, many groups and individuals came out against the new law. Among them were several southern clergymen, who felt religion was the province of churches, not schools, and also many local business organizations, which feared that a blow to science education might discourage lucrative high-tech companies from migrating to Arkansas. With the aid of the ACLU, which had been instrumental in the Scopes case, they challenged Act 590 on the grounds that it violated the doctrine of separation of church and state, that it infringed on teachers' academic freedom, and that the law was vague from a legal standpoint.

These arguments against Act 590 eventually won out. On January 5, 1982, the judge hearing the case ruled that "Creation-science" was religion, not science, and could not be taught in public classrooms. The state of Arkansas did not appeal the decision. Later, in 1987, the U.S. Supreme Court made an almost identical ruling that struck down a pro-creationist act that had recently passed in Louisiana.

But despite these setbacks, advocates of creationism remained active. In the 1990s, as they continued their efforts to gain equal time with evolutionists, some conservative politicians aided them with supportive public statements. Early in 1996 Republican presidential hopeful Pat Buchanan told an ABC reporter that parents had a right to insist that "Godless evolution" not be taught to their children. In March 1996 the Tennessee legislature considered a bill that would require school boards to dismiss teachers who present evolution as a scientific fact. And in Alabama, creationists successfully pushed to get biology textbooks to include a disclaimer saying that evolution is a "controversial theory" that only "some scientists" accept. Thus, the controversy that Charles Darwin ignited in 1859, and which flared up again in the 1925 Scopes trial, continues to smolder.

The Evolutionary Synthesis

During these many decades of bickering between evolutionists and creationists, reputable scientists did not even slightly doubt that evolution was a fact. Although it was and still is labeled a theory, scientists define the term "theory" quite differently than the anti-evolutionists do. To the latter, a theory is simply an assumption, a speculation, or an educated guess based on little or no evidence; but in science, a theory is an organized, usually quite complex system of principles that seems to predict and explain a wide variety of observ-

Conservative politician Pat Buchanan, seen here during one of his unsuccessful runs for president, has spoken out against teaching evolution in schools.

able phenomena in a believable way. For instance, the theory of universal gravitation correctly predicts and accounts for the mutual attractions of material objects, both on earth and throughout the observable universe; and no one doubts that the force of gravity is real simply because it is labeled a theory.

That does not mean, however, that science has always accepted all of the ideas that Darwin presented in his *Origin of Species*. While the book was instrumental in the scientific community's general acceptance of the doctrine of evolution, a number of experts long argued over which details Darwin got right and which he got wrong. The central bone of contention was the principle of natural selection, which presupposed a natural world ruled by blind, often cruel chance. "The Victorians [inhabitants of Britain in the late 1800s] had difficulties with natural selection," Peter Bowler explains,

> because they could not accept the idea of undirected evolution. Darwin's theory had been published at the right time to tip the balance in favor of exploring the general concept of evolution, but most of his followers decided that there must be something more purposeful than natural selection in control.

Biologist Julian Huxley, grandson of the great Thomas H. Huxley, interacts with a chimp. The younger Huxley helped to confirm many of Darwin's ideas.

> For every evolutionist who followed Darwin in the study of adaptation . . . there were dozens who preferred to concentrate on the grand sweep of progress up to mankind revealed in the fossil record.[53]

As a result, in the late nineteenth and early twentieth centuries, biologists and other scientists advanced a number of alternate hypotheses for the mechanism directing evolution. The emergence of the biological subscience of genetics in the early 1900s, for example, at first seemed to promise an answer. Perhaps, some scientists proposed, the part played in the process of heredity by the genes might constitute a workable alternative to natural selection. In particular, they suggested, sudden, large-scale mutations of the genes might be the key factor in bringing about new species. By contrast, Darwin had argued that smaller mutations, happening more gradually, are more crucial in the evolutionary process.

In time, researchers came to realize that large-scale mutations are harmful and that Darwin had been right about smaller ones being responsible for most positive evolutionary change. Furthermore, it became clear that mutation itself is not the chief source of variations in the genes. Instead, a complex recombination of the genetic material produces the majority of change in both individuals and species. But there had to be some process choosing or affecting which genetic combinations are successful and perpetuated and which are not. After careful study of a mountain of evidence that grew (and today continues to grow) larger by the year, the experts realized that natural selection is the only credible process capable of controlling the flow of genes through a population of animals or plants.

In the late 1930s and on into the 1940s, therefore, Darwin's theory of natural selection and the new science of genetics were reconciled in what became known as the "evolutionary synthesis" (a term coined

Natural Selection as a Part of Evolution

In this excerpt from his book Evolution and the Myth of Creationism, *zoologist Tim M. Berra explains the relationship between natural selection and evolution as presently understood by scientists.*

"Some genetic variants may be better adapted to their environment than others of their sort, and will therefore tend to survive to maturity and to leave more offspring than will organisms with less favorable variations. This 'differential reproduction' of genetic variants is the modern definition of natural selection. It results in a change in the frequency of occurrence of certain genes over time within a population [of plants or animals]—more of some genes, fewer of others. Changes of this sort, and their manifold consequences as the generations come and go, constitute the definition of evolution. In summary, *evolution is a change of gene frequency* brought about by natural selection (differential reproduction) and other processes acting upon the variations produced by sexual reproduction, mutation, and other mechanisms. The environment is the selecting agent, and because the environment changes over time and from one region to another, different variants will be selected under different environmental conditions. The Canada of the ice age was a different environment than the Canada of today."

in 1942 by leading biologist Julian Huxley, grandson of Darwin's friend T. H. Huxley). Among the key and now classic studies in this vein were Theodosius Dobzhansky's *Genetics and the Origin of Species* (1937), Julian Huxley's *Evolution: The Modern Synthesis* (1942), Ernst Mayr's *Systematics and the Origin of Species* (1942), George Gaylord Simpson's *Tempo and Mode in Evolution* (1944) and *The Meaning of Evolution* (1949), and G. L. Stebbins's *Variation and Evolution in Plants* (1950).

Humanity Placed in Truer Perspective

That Darwin had been essentially right all along about natural selection was striking enough to most scientists and other educated people. Even more amazing was that his evolutionary theory also correctly foresaw the character of later discoveries about human origins. For years most scientists had clung to the notion that evolution had to be somehow driven toward the formation of advanced intelligence, as personified in humans. It seemed to them that the evolutionary process was inherently progressive. In other words, no matter where or when it occurred and under whatever conditions, it strove for increased complexity and was therefore bound, sooner or later, to result in the ultimate natural creation—the human brain. In contrast, Darwin had argued that evolution was random, without any inherent direction or purpose. And the twentieth century witnessed the discovery of widespread physical evidence that he was right. Numerous fossils of early humanlike creatures found in Africa, Bowler writes, have

> confirmed Darwin's original prediction that our ancestors stood upright *before* the great expansion of the human brain began. The separation of the human family [from lower orders of mammals] was the product of an adaptive modification, not the inevitable outcome of a trend toward bigger brains. Far from being a predictable goal of evolution, the human race now appears to be the unlikely outcome of a chapter of lucky accidents. Of all the nineteenth-century evolutionists, Darwin was the only one who even partially anticipated such a radical conclusion.[54]

One of the great achievements of Darwin and his *Origin of Species*, therefore, was to put humanity's place in nature in truer perspective. To be sure, a number of people are not yet ready to accept the notion that humans are not the central and special product of creation. But the history of modern science and society shows how time and again new scientific concepts have at first seemed incredible, disturbing, and/or blasphemous; yet in the fullness of time, as over-whelming evidence testified to their truth, they became universally accepted. "In 1859," comments noted zoologist Tim M. Berra,

> Darwin completed the Copernican revolution by removing humans from center stage. . . . It is just a matter of time before [the] fruitful concept [of evolution] comes to be accepted by the public as wholeheartedly as it has accepted the spherical Earth and the Sun-centered solar system.[55]

Excerpt from Darwin's *Origin of Species*

This is the third chapter of Darwin's masterpiece, *The Origin of Species*, as it appeared for the first time in 1859. In the tract, the author explains and gives examples of the "struggle for existence," his name for the natural competition in which plants and animals fight to survive, thereby setting in motion the process of natural selection, which allows the strongest among them to survive and pass on their superior traits to their offspring. For its conceptual brilliance, logical and precise organization and presentation, and clarity of expression, this excerpt stands on its own as one of the greatest scientific writings of all time. Note also how Darwin frequently and very graciously and professionally gives credit to others whose ideas and data he has drawn on. These include, among others, philosopher Herbert Spencer, horticulturalist W. Herbert, geologist Charles Lyell, botanists Augustin-Pyrame de Candolle and Hugh Falconer, and economist Thomas Malthus.

Chapter 3: Struggle For Existence

Its bearing on natural selection—The term used in a wide sense—Geometrical ratio of increase—Rapid increase of naturalised animals and plants——Nature of the checks in increase—Competition universal—Effects of climate—Protection from the number of individuals——Complex relations of all animals and plants throughout nature—Struggle for life most severe between individuals and varieties of the same species: often severe between species of the same genus—The relation of organism to organism the most important of all relations.

Before entering on the subject of this chapter, I must make a few preliminary remarks, to show how the struggle for existence bears on Natural Selection. It has been seen in the last chapter that amongst organic beings in a state of nature there is some individual variability: indeed I am not aware that this has ever been disputed. It is immaterial for us whether a multitude of doubtful forms be called species or sub-species or varieties; what rank, for instance, the two or three hundred doubtful forms of British plants are entitled to hold, if the existence of any well-marked varieties be admitted. But the mere existence of individual variability and of some few well-marked varieties, though necessary as the foundation for the work, helps us but little in understanding how species arise in nature. How have all those exquisite adaptations of one part of the organisation to another part, and to the conditions of life, and of one organic being to another being, been perfected? We see these beautiful co-adaptations most plainly in the woodpecker and the mistletoe; and only a little less plainly in the humblest parasite which clings to the hairs of a quadruped or feathers of a bird; in the structure of the beetle which dives through the water; in the plumed seed which is wafted by the gentlest breeze; in short, we see beautiful adaptations everywhere and in every part of the organic world.

Again, it may be asked, how is it that varieties, which I have called incipient species, become ultimately converted into good and distinct species which in most cases obviously differ from each other far more than do the varieties of the same species? How do those groups of species, which constitute what are called distinct genera, and which differ from each other more than do the species of the same genus, arise? All these results, as we shall more fully see in the next chapter, follow from the struggle for life. Owing to this struggle, variations, however slight and from whatever cause proceeding, if they be in any degree profitable to the individuals of a species, in their infinitely complex relations to other organic beings and to their physical conditions of life, will tend to the preservation of such individuals, and will generally be inherited by the offspring. The offspring, also, will thus have a better chance of surviving, for, of the many individuals of any species which are periodically born, but a small number can survive. I have called this principle, by which each slight variation, if useful, is preserved, by the term Natural Selection, in order to mark its relation to man's power of selection. But the expression often used by Mr. Herbert Spencer of the Survival of the Fittest is more accurate, and is sometimes equally convenient. We have seen that man by selection can certainly produce great results, and can adapt organic beings to his own uses, through the accumulation of slight but useful variations, given to him by the hand of Nature. But Natural Selection, as we shall hereafter see, is a power incessantly ready for action, and is as immeasurably superior to man's feeble efforts, as the works of Nature are to those of Art.

We will now discuss in a little more detail the struggle for existence. In my future work this subject will be treated, as it well deserves, at greater length. The elder De Candolle and Lyell have largely and philosophically shown that all organic beings are exposed to severe competition. In regard to plants, no one has treated this subject with more spirit and ability than W. Herbert, Dean of Manchester, evidently the result of his great horticultural knowledge. Nothing is easier than to admit in words the truth of the universal struggle for life, or more difficult—at least I have found it so—than constantly to bear this conclusion in mind. Yet unless it be thoroughly engrained in the mind, the whole economy of nature, with every fact on distribution, rarity, abundance, extinction, and variation, will be dimly seen or quite misunderstood. We behold the face of nature bright with gladness, we often see superabundance of food; we do not see or we forget, that the birds which are idly singing round us mostly live on insects or seeds, and are thus constantly destroying life; or we forget how largely these songsters, or their eggs, or their nestlings, are destroyed by birds and beasts of prey; we do not always bear in mind, that, though food may be now superabundant, it is not so at all seasons of each recurring year.

The Term, Struggle for Existence, Used in a Large Sense
I should premise that I use this term in a large and metaphorical sense including dependence of one being on another, and including (which is more important) not only the life of the individual, but success in leaving progeny. Two canine animals, in a time of dearth, may be truly said to struggle with each other which shall get food and live. But a plant on the edge of a desert is said to struggle for life against the drought, though more properly it should be said to be dependent on the moisture. A plant which annually produces a thousand seeds, of which only one of an average comes to maturity, may be more truly said to struggle with the plants of the same and other kinds which already clothe the ground. The mistletoe is dependent on the apple and a few other trees, but can only in a far-fetched sense be said to struggle with these trees, for, if too many of these parasites grow on the same tree, it languishes and dies. But several seedling mistletoes, growing close together on the same branch, may more truly

be said to struggle with each other. As the mistletoe is disseminated by birds, its existence depends on them; and it may methodically be said to struggle with other fruit-bearing plants, in tempting the birds to devour and thus disseminate its seeds. In these several senses, which pass into each other, I use for convenience' sake the general term of Struggle for Existence.

Geometrical Ratio of Increase

A struggle for existence inevitably follows from the high rate at which all organic beings tend to increase. Every being, which during its natural lifetime produces several eggs or seeds, must suffer destruction during some period of its life, and during some season or occasional year, otherwise, on the principle of geometrical increase, its numbers would quickly become so inordinately great that no country could support the product. Hence, as more individuals are produced than can possibly survive, there must in every case be a struggle for existence, either one individual with another of the same species, or with the individuals of distinct species, or with the physical conditions of life. It is the doctrine of Malthus applied with manifold force to the whole animal and vegetable kingdoms; for in this case there can be no artificial increase of food, and no prudential restraint from marriage. Although some species may be now increasing, more or less rapidly, in numbers, all cannot do so, for the world would not hold them.

There is no exception to the rule that every organic being naturally increases at so high a rate, that, if not destroyed, the earth would soon be covered by the progeny of a single pair. Even slow-breeding man has doubled in twenty-five years, and at this rate, in less than a thousand years, there would literally not be standing-room for his progeny. Linnaeus has calculated that if an annual plant produced only two seeds—and there is no plant so unproductive as this—and their seedlings next year produced two, and so on, then in twenty years there should be a million plants. The elephant is reckoned the slowest breeder of all known animals, and I have taken some pains to estimate its probable minimum rate of natural increase; it will be safest to assume that it begins breeding when thirty years old, and goes on breeding till ninety years old, bringing forth six young in the interval, and surviving till one hundred years old; if this be so, after a period of from

740 to 750 years there would be nearly nineteen million elephants alive, descended from the first pair.

But we have better evidence on this subject than mere theoretical calculations, namely, the numerous recorded cases of the astonishingly rapid increase of various animals in a state of nature, when circumstances have been favourable to them during two or three following seasons. Still more striking is the evidence from our domestic animals of many kinds which have run wild in several parts of the world; if the statements of the rate of increase of slow-breeding cattle and horses in South America, and latterly in Australia, had not been well authenticated, they would have been incredible. So it is with plants; cases could be given of introduced plants which have become common throughout whole islands in a period of less than ten years. Several of the plants, such as the cardoon and a tall thistle, which are now the commonest over the whole plains of La Plata, clothing square leagues of surface almost to the exclusion of every other plant, have been introduced from Europe; and there are plants which now range in India, as I hear from Dr. Falconer, from Cape Comorin to the Himalaya, which have been imported from America since its discovery. In such cases, and endless others could be given, no one supposes, that the fertility of the animals or plants has been suddenly and temporarily increased in any sensible degree. The obvious explanation is that the conditions of life have been highly favourable, and that there has consequently been less destruction of the old and young, and that nearly all the young have been enabled to breed. Their geometrical ratio of increase, the result of which never fails to be surprising, simply explains their extraordinarily rapid increase and wide diffusion in their new homes.

In a state of nature almost every full-grown plant annually produces seed, and amongst animals there are very few which do not annually pair. Hence we may confidently assert, that all plants and animals are tending to increase at a geometrical ratio,—that all would rapidly stock every station in which they could anyhow exist,—and that this geometrical tendency to increase must be checked by destruction at some period of life. Our familiarity with the larger domestic animals tends, I think, to mislead us: we see no great destruction falling on them, but we do not keep in mind that thousands are annually slaughtered for food, and that in a state of nature an equal number would have somehow to be disposed of.

The only difference between organisms which annually produce eggs or seeds by the thousand, and those which produce extremely few, is, that the slow-breeders would require a few more years to people, under favourable conditions, a whole district, let it be ever so large. The condor lays a couple of eggs and the ostrich a score, and yet in the same country the condor may be the more numerous of the two; the Fulmar petrel lays but one egg, yet it is believed to be the most numerous bird in the world. One fly deposits hundreds of eggs, and another, like the hippobosca, a single one; but this difference does not determine how many individuals of the two species can be supported in a district. A large number of eggs is of some importance to those species which depend on a fluctuating amount of food, for it allows them rapidly to increase in number. But the real importance of a large number of eggs or seeds is to make up for much destruction at some period of life; and this period in the great majority of cases is an early one. If an animal can in any way protect its own eggs or young, a small number may be produced, and yet the average stock be fully kept up; but if many eggs or young are destroyed, many must be produced, or the species will become extinct. It would suffice to keep up the full number of a tree, which lived on an average for a thousand years, if a single seed were produced once in a thousand years, supposing that this seed were never destroyed, and could be ensured to germinate in a fitting place. So that, in all cases, the average number of any animal or plant depends only indirectly on the number of its eggs or seeds.

In looking at Nature, it is most necessary to keep the foregoing considerations always in mind—never to forget that every single organic being may be said to be striving to the utmost to increase in numbers; that each lives by a struggle at some period of its life; that heavy destruction inevitably falls either on the young or old, during each generation or at recurrent intervals. Lighten any check, mitigate the destruction ever so little, and the number of the species will almost instantaneously increase to any amount.

Nature of the Checks to Increase
The causes which check the natural tendency of each species to increase are most obscure. Look at the most vigorous

species; by as much as it swarms in numbers, by so much will it tend to increase still further. We know not exactly what the checks are even in a single instance. Nor will this surprise any one who reflects how ignorant we are on this head, even in regard to mankind, although so incomparably better known than any other animal. This subject of the checks to increase has been ably treated by several authors, and I hope in a future work to discuss it at considerable length, more especially in regard to the feral animals of South America. Here I will make only a few remarks, just to recall to the reader's mind some of the chief points. Eggs or very young animals seem generally to suffer most, but this is not invariably the case. With plants there is a vast destruction of seeds, but, from some observations which I have made it appears that the seedlings suffer most from germinating in ground already thickly stocked with other plants. Seedlings, also, are destroyed in vast numbers by various enemies; for instance, on a piece of ground three feet long and two wide, dug and cleared, and where there could be no choking from other plants, I marked all the seedlings of our native weeds as they came up, and out of 357 no less than 295 were destroyed, chiefly by slugs and insects. If turf which has long been mown, and the case would be the same with turf closely browsed by quadrupeds, be let to grow, the more vigorous plants gradually kill the less vigorous, though fully grown plants; thus out of twenty species growing on a little plot of mown turf (three feet by four) nine species perished, from the other species being allowed to grow up freely.

The amount of food for each species of course gives the extreme limit to which each can increase; but very frequently it is not the obtaining food, but the serving as prey to other animals, which determines the average numbers of a species. Thus, there seems to be little doubt that the stock of partridges, grouse, and hares on any large estate depends chiefly on the destruction of vermin. If not one head of game were shot during the next twenty years in England, and, at the same time, if no vermin were destroyed, there would, in all probability, be less game than at present, although hundreds of thousands of game animals are now annually shot. On the other hand, in some cases, as with the elephant, none are destroyed by beasts of prey; for even the tiger in India most rarely dares to attack a young elephant protected by its dam.

Climate plays an important part in determining the average number of a species, and periodical seasons of extreme cold or drought seem to be the most effective of all checks. I estimated (chiefly from the greatly reduced numbers of nests in the spring) that the winter of 1854–5 destroyed four-fifths of the birds in my own grounds; and this is a tremendous destruction, when we remember that ten per cent is an extraordinarily severe mortality from epidemics with man. The action of climate seems at first sight to be quite independent of the struggle for existence; but in so far as climate chiefly acts in reducing food, it brings on the most severe struggle between the individuals, whether of the same or of distinct species, which subsist on the same kind of food. Even when climate, for instance, extreme cold, acts directly, it will be the least vigorous individuals, or those which have got least food through the advancing winter, which will suffer most. When we travel from south to north, or from a damp region to a dry, we invariably see some species gradually getting rarer and rarer, and finally disappearing; and the change of climate being conspicuous, we are tempted to attribute the whole effect to its direct action. But this is a false view; we forget that each species, even where it most abounds, is constantly suffering enormous destruction at some period of its life, from enemies or from competitors for the same place and food; and if these enemies or competitors be in the least degree favoured by any slight change of climate, they will increase in numbers; and as each area is already fully stocked with inhabitants, the other species must decrease. When we travel southward and see a species decreasing in numbers, we may feel sure that the cause lies quite as much in other species being favoured, as in this one being hurt. So it is when we travel northward, but in a somewhat lesser degree, for the number of species of all kinds, and therefore of competitors, decreases northwards; hence in going northwards, or in ascending a mountain, we far oftener meet with stunted forms, due to the directly injurious action of climate, than we do in proceeding southwards or in descending a mountain. When we reach the Arctic regions, or snow-capped summits, or absolute deserts, the struggle for life is almost exclusively with the elements.

That climate acts in main part indirectly by favouring other species, we clearly see in the prodigious number of plants which in our gardens can perfectly well endure our climate, but which never become naturalised, for they cannot compete with our native plants nor resist destruction by our native animals.

When a species, owing to highly favourable circumstances, increases inordinately in numbers in a small tract, epidemics—at least, this seems generally to occur with our game animals—often ensue; and here we have a limiting check independent of the struggle for life. But even some of these so-called epidemics appear to be due to parasitic worms, which have from some cause, possibly in part through facility of diffusion amongst the crowded animals, been disproportionally favoured: and here comes in a sort of struggle between the parasite and its prey.

On the other hand, in many cases, a large stock of individuals of the same species, relatively to the numbers of its enemies, is absolutely necessary for its preservation. Thus we can easily raise plenty of corn and rape-seed, &c., in our fields, because the seeds are in great excess compared with the number of birds which feed on them; nor can the birds, though having a super-abundance of food at this one season, increase in number proportionally to the supply of seed, as their numbers are checked during the winter; but any one who has tried, knows how troublesome it is to get seed from a few wheat or other such plants in a garden: I have in this case lost every single seed. This view of the necessity of a large stock of the same species for its preservation, explains, I believe, some singular facts in nature such as that of very rare plants being sometimes extremely abundant, in the few spots where they do exist; and that of some social plants being social, that is abounding in individuals, even on the extreme verge of their range. For in such cases, we may believe, that a plant could exist only where the conditions of its life were so favourable that many could exist together, and thus save the species from utter destruction. I should add that the good effects of intercrossing, and the ill effects of close interbreeding, no doubt come into play in many of these cases; but I will not here enlarge on this subject.

Complex Relations of All Animals and Plants to Each Other in the Struggle for Existence

Many cases are on record showing how complex and unexpected are the checks and relations between organic beings, which have to struggle together in the same country. I will give only a single instance, which, though a simple one, interested me. In Staffordshire, on the estate of a relation, where I had ample means of investigation, there was a large and extremely barren heath, which had never been touched by the hand of man; but several hundred acres of exactly the same nature had been enclosed twenty-five years previously and planted with Scotch fir. The change in the native vegetation of the planted part of the heath was most remarkable, more than is generally seen in passing from one quite different soil to another: not only the proportional numbers of the heath-plants were wholly changed, but twelve species of plants (not counting grasses and carices) flourished in the plantations, which could not be found on the heath. The effect on the insects must have been still greater, for six insectivorous birds were very common in the plantations, which were not to be seen on the heath; and the heath was frequented by two or three distinct insectivorous birds. Here we see how potent has been the effect of the introduction of a single tree, nothing whatever else having been done, with the exception of the land having been enclosed, so that cattle could not enter. But how important an element enclosure is, I plainly saw near Farnham, in Surrey. Here there are extensive heaths, with a few clumps of old Scotch firs on the distant hilltops: within the last ten years large spaces have been enclosed, and self-sown firs are now springing up in multitudes, so close together that all cannot live. When I ascertained that these young trees had not been sown or planted, I was so much surprised at their numbers that I went to several points of view, whence I could examine hundreds of acres of the unenclosed heath, and literally I could not see a single Scotch fir, except the old planted clumps. But on looking closely between the stems of the heath, I found a multitude of seedlings and little trees which had been perpetually browsed down by the cattle. In one square yard, at a point some hundred yards distant from one of the old clumps, I counted thirty-two little trees; and one of them, with twenty-six rings of growth, had during many years tried to raise its head above the stems of the heath, and had failed. No wonder that, as soon as the land was enclosed, it became thickly clothed with vigorously growing young firs. Yet the heath was so extremely barren and so extensive that no one would ever have imagined that cattle would have so closely and effectually searched it for food.

Here we see that cattle absolutely determine the existence of the Scotch fir; but in several parts of the world insects determine the existence of cattle. Perhaps Paraguay offers the most curious instance of this; for here neither cattle nor horses nor dogs have ever run wild, though they swarm southward and northward in a feral state; and Azara and Rengger have shown that this is caused by the greater number in Paraguay of a certain fly, which lays its eggs in the navels of these animals when first born. The increase of these flies, numerous as they are, must be habitually checked by some means, probably by other parasitic insects. Hence, if certain insectivorous birds were to decrease in Paraguay, the parasitic insects would probably increase; and this would lessen the number of the navel-frequenting flies—then cattle and horses would become feral, and this would certainly greatly alter (as indeed I have observed in parts of South America) the vegetation: this again would largely affect the insects; and this, as we have just seen in Staffordshire, the insectivorous birds, and so onwards in ever-increasing circles of complexity. Not that under nature the relations will ever be as simple as this. Battle within battle must be continually recurring with varying success; and yet in the long-run the forces are so nicely balanced, that the face of nature remains for long periods of time uniform, though assuredly the merest trifle would give the victory to one organic being over another. Nevertheless, so profound is our ignorance, and so high our presumption, that we marvel when we hear of the extinction of an organic being; and as we do not see the cause, we invoke cataclysms to desolate the world, or invent laws on the duration of the forms of life!

I am tempted to give one more instance showing how plants and animals remote in the scale of nature, are bound together by a web of complex relations. I shall hereafter have occasion to show that the exotic Lobelia fulgens is never visited in my garden by insects, and consequently, from its peculiar structure, never sets a seed. Nearly all our orchidaceous plants absolutely require the visits of insects to remove their pollen-masses and thus to fertilise them. I find from experiments that humble-bees are almost indispensable to the fertilisation of the heartsease (Viola tricolor), for other bees do not visit this flower. I have also found that the visits of bees are necessary for the fertilisation of some kinds of clover; for instance, 20 heads of Dutch clover (Trifolium repens) yielded 2,290 seeds, but 20 other heads protected from bees produced not one. Again, 100 heads of red clover (T. pratense) produced 2,700 seeds, but the same number of protected heads produced not a single seed. Humble-bees alone visit red clover, as other bees cannot reach the nectar. It has been suggested that moths may fertilise the clovers; but I doubt whether they could do so in the case of the red clover, from their weight not being sufficient to depress the wing petals. Hence we may infer as highly probable that, if the whole genus of humble-bees became extinct or very rare in England, the heartsease and red clover would become vary rare, or wholly disappear. The number of humble-bees in any district depends in a great measure upon the number of field-mice, which destroy their combs and nests; and Col. Newman, who has long attended to the habits of humble-bees, believes that "more than two-thirds of them are thus destroyed all over England." Now the number of mice is largely dependent, as every one knows, on the number of cats; and Col. Newman says, "Near villages and small towns I have found the nests of humble-bees more numerous than elsewhere, which I attribute to the number of cats that destroy the mice." Hence it is quite credible that the presence of a feline animal in large numbers in a district might determine, through the intervention first of mice and then of bees, the frequency of certain flowers in that district!

In the case of every species, many different checks, acting at different periods of life, and during different seasons or years, probably come into play; some one check or some few being generally the most potent; but all will concur in determining the average number or even the existence of the species. In some cases it can be shown that widely-different checks act on the same species in different districts. When we look at the plants and bushes clothing an entangled bank, we are tempted to attribute their proportional numbers and kinds to what we call chance. But how false a view is this! Every one has heard that when an American forest is cut down a very different vegetation springs up; but it has been observed that ancient Indian ruins in the Southern United States, which must formerly have been cleared of trees, now display the same beautiful diversity and proportion of kinds as in the surrounding virgin forest. What a struggle must have gone on during long centuries between the several kinds of trees each annually scattering its seeds by the thousand; what war between insect and insect—between insects, snails, and other animals with birds and beasts of prey—all striving to increase, all feeding on each other, or on the trees, their seeds and seedlings, or on the other plants which first clothed the ground and thus checked the growth of the trees! Throw up a handful of feathers, and all fall to the ground according to definite laws; but how simple is the problem where each shall fall compared to that of the action and reaction of the innumerable plants and animals which have determined, in the course of centuries, the proportional numbers and kinds of trees now growing on the old Indian ruins!

The dependency of one organic being on another, as of a parasite on its prey, lies generally between beings remote in the scale of nature. This is likewise sometimes the case with those which may be strictly said to struggle with each other for existence, as in the case of locusts and grass-feeding quadrupeds. But the struggle will almost invariably be most severe between the individuals of the same species, for they frequent the same districts, require the same food, and are exposed to the same dangers. In the case of varieties of the same species, the struggle will generally be almost equally severe, and we sometimes see the contest soon decided: for instance, if several varieties of wheat be sown together, and the mixed seed be resown, some of the varieties which best suit the soil or climate, or are naturally the most fertile, will beat the others and so yield more seed, and will consequently in a few years supplant the other varieties. To keep up a mixed stock of even such extremely close varieties as the variously-coloured sweet peas, they must be each year harvested separately, and the seed then mixed in due proportion, otherwise the weaker kinds will steadily decrease in number and disappear. So again with the varieties of sheep; it has been asserted that certain mountain-varieties will starve out other mountain-varieties, so that they cannot be kept together. The same result has followed from keeping together different varieties of the medicinal leech. It may even be doubted whether the varieties of any of our domestic plants or animals have so exactly the same strength, habits, and constitution, that the original proportions of a mixed stock (crossing being prevented) could be kept up for half-a-dozen generations, if they were allowed to struggle together, in the same manner as beings in a state of nature, and if the seed or young were not annually preserved in due proportion.

Struggle for Life Most Severe Between Individuals and Varieties of the Same Species

As the species of the same genus usually have, though by no means invariably, much similarity in habits and constitution, and always in structure, the struggle will generally be more severe between them, if they come into competition with each other, than between the species of distinct genera. We see this in the recent extension over parts of the United States of one species of swallow having caused the decrease of another species. The recent increase of the missel-thrush in parts of Scotland has caused the decrease of the song-thrush. How frequently we hear of one species of rat taking the place of another species under the most different climates! In Russia the small Asiatic cockroach has everywhere driven before it its great congener. In Australia the imported hive-bee is rapidly exterminating the small, stingless native bee. One species of charlock has been known to supplant another species; and so in other cases. We can dimly see why the competition should be most severe between allied forms, which fill nearly the same place in the economy of nature; but probably in no one case could we precisely say why one species has been victorious over another in the great battle of life.

A corollary of the highest importance may be deduced from the foregoing remarks, namely, that the structure of every organic being is related, in the most essential yet often hidden manner, to that of all the other organic beings, with which it comes into competition for food or residence, or from which it has to escape, or on which it preys. This is obvious in the structure of the teeth and talons of the tiger; and in that of the legs and claws of the parasite which clings to the hair on the tiger's body. But in the beautifully plumed seed of the dandelion, and in the flattened and fringed legs of the water-beetle, the relation seems at first confined to the elements of air and water. Yet the advantage of plumed seeds no doubt stands in the closest relation to the land being already thickly clothed with other plants; so that the seeds may be widely distributed and fall on unoccupied ground. In the water-beetle, the structure of its legs, so well adapted for diving, allows it to compete with other aquatic insects, to hunt for its own prey, and to escape serving as prey to other animals.

The store of nutriment laid up within the seeds of many plants seems at first to have no sort of relation to other plants. But from the strong growth of young plants produced from such seeds, as peas and beans, when sown in the midst of long grass, it may be suspected that the chief use of the nutriment in the seed is to favour the growth of the seedlings, whilst struggling with other plants growing vigorously all around.

Look at a plant in the midst of its range, why does it not double or quadruple its numbers? We know that it can perfectly well withstand a little more heat or cold, dampness or dryness, for elsewhere it ranges into slightly hotter or colder, damper or drier districts. In this case we can clearly see that if we wish in imagination to give the plant the power of increasing in number, we should have to give it some advantage over its competitors, or over the animals which prey on it. On the confines of its geographical range, a change of constitution with respect to climate would clearly be an advantage to our plant; but we have reason to believe that only a few plants or animals range so far, that they are destroyed exclusively by the rigour of the climate. Not until we reach the extreme confines of life, in the Arctic regions or on the borders of an utter desert, will competition cease. The land may be extremely cold or dry, yet there will be competition between some few species, or between the individuals of the same species, for the warmest or dampest spots.

Hence we can see that when a plant or animal is placed in a new country amongst new competitors, the conditions of its life will generally be changed in an essential manner, although the climate may be exactly the same as in its former home. If its average numbers are to increase in its new home, we should have to modify it in a different way to what we should have had to do in its native country; for we should have to give it some advantage over a different set of competitors or enemies.

It is good thus to try in imagination to give to any one species an advantage over another. Probably in no single instance should we know what to do. This ought to convince us of our ignorance on the mutual relations of all organic beings; a conviction as necessary, as it is difficult to acquire. All that we can do, is to keep steadily in mind that each organic being is striving to increase in a geometrical ratio; that each at some period of its life, during some season of the year, during each generation or at intervals, has to struggle for life and to suffer great destruction. When we reflect on this struggle, we may console ourselves with the full belief, that the war of nature is not incessant, that no fear is felt, that death is generally prompt, and that the vigorous, the healthy, and the happy survive and multiply.

Source Notes

Introduction: The Two Revolutions of Darwin's Masterwork

1. Robert Wesson, *Beyond Natural Selection*. Cambridge: MIT Press, 1991, p. 6.
2. Peter J. Bowler, *Charles Darwin: The Man and His Influence*. New York: Cambridge University Press, 1990, p. 220.
3. Bowler, *Charles Darwin*, p. 220.

Chapter 1: An Eager Young Naturalist on a Voyage of Discovery

4. Charles Darwin, *Autobiography*, in *The Autobiography of Charles Darwin and Selected Letters*. Edited by Francis Darwin. New York: Dover Publications, 1958, p. 9.
5. Darwin, *Autobiography*, p. 10.
6. Darwin, *Autobiography*, p. 11.
7. Darwin, *Autobiography*, p. 9.
8. The second half of this paragraph quoted from Don Nardo, *Charles Darwin*. New York: Chelsea House, 1993, p. 27.
9. Darwin, *Autobiography*, p. 22.
10. Darwin, *Autobiography*, p. 24.
11. The second half of this paragraph quoted from Nardo, *Charles Darwin*, p. 31.
12. Quoted in Francis Darwin, ed., *The Life and Letters of Charles Darwin*. 3 vols. 1885. Reprint, New York: Basic Books, 1959, vol. 1, pp. 208–10.
13. The second half of this paragraph quoted from Nardo, *Charles Darwin*, pp. 17–19.
14. Charles Darwin, *The Origin of Species by Means of Natural Selection, or, The Preservation of Favored Races in the Struggle for Life*. 1859. Reprint, New York: New American Library, 1958, pp. 276–77.
15. Darwin, *Autobiography*, pp. 28–29.

Chapter 2: Darwin's Grand Theory: From Conception to Written Manuscript

16. Darwin, *Autobiography*, p. 42.
17. Darwin, *Autobiography*, p. 43.
18. Daniel C. Dennett, *Darwin's Dangerous Idea: Evolution and the Meanings of Life*. New York: Simon & Schuster, 1995, pp. 40–41.
19. Darwin, *Origin of Species*, p. 128.

20. Most of this paragraph quoted from Nardo, *Charles Darwin*, pp. 66–67.
21. Quoted in John Bowlby, *Charles Darwin: A New Life*. New York: W. W. Norton, 1990, p. 331.
22. Parts of this and the preceding two paragraphs quoted from Nardo, *Charles Darwin*, pp. 76–78.
23. Quoted in *The Life and Letters of Charles Darwin*, vol. 2, p. 216.

Chapter 3: Before *Origin*: Pre-Darwinian Theories of Evolution

24. Quoted in Richard Dawkins, *The Blind Watchmaker: Why the Evidence of Evolution Reveals a Universe Without Design*. New York: W. W. Norton, 1987, p. 5.
25. Bowler, *Charles Darwin*, p. 19.
26. Quoted in Philip Wheelwright, ed., *The Presocratics*. New York: Macmillan, 1966, p. 58.
27. Quoted in Lucretius, *The Nature of the Universe*. Translated by Ronald Latham. Baltimore: Penguin Books, 1951, p. 197.
28. Bentley Glass, "The Eighteenth Century," in *Forerunners of Darwin: 1745–1859*. Edited by Bentley Glass et al., eds., Baltimore: Johns Hopkins University Press, 1968, p. 60.
29. Quoted in Glass, *Forerunners of Darwin*, p. 77.
30. Quoted in Desmond King-Hele, *Erasmus Darwin*. New York: Scribner's, 1963, pp. 67–68.
31. Quoted in King-Hele, *Erasmus Darwin*, p. 69.
32. Bowler, *Charles Darwin*, pp. 20–21.
33. Quoted in King-Hele, *Erasmus Darwin*, pp. 78–79.
34. Darwin, *Autobiography*, p. 49.
35. Bowler, *Charles Darwin*, pp. 23–24.
36. Bowler, *Charles Darwin*, p. 23.

Chapter 4: Darwin's Book Receives a Loud and Mixed Reception

37. Darwin, *Origin of Species*, pp. 443–44.
38. Quoted in Gertrude Himmelfarb, *Darwin and the Darwinian Revolution*. New York: W. W. Norton, 1959, p. 242.
39. Quoted in Himmelfarb, *Darwin and the Darwinian Revolution*, p. 245.
40. Himmelfarb, *Darwin and the Darwinian Revolution*, pp. 244–48.
41. Quoted in Leonard Huxley, *Life and Letters of Thomas Henry Huxley*. 2 vols. New York: Appleton, 1900, vol. 1, p. 184.
42. Tom McGowen, *The Great Monkey Trial: Science vs. Fundamentalism in America*. New York: Franklin Watts, 1990, pp. 21–22.
43. Joseph D. Hooker, review of Darwin's *Origin of Species* in *Gardener's Chronicle*, December 31, 1859.

44. Quoted in *Autobiography of Charles Darwin and Selected Letters*, p. 267.

45. Quoted in the *Spectator*, April 7, 1860.

46. Quoted in *Autobiography of Charles Darwin and Selected Letters*, p. 253.

47. Quoted in William Irvine, *Apes, Angels, & Victorians: The Story of Darwin, Huxley, and Evolution*. New York: McGraw-Hill, 1955, p. 240.

48. Quoted in Darwin, *The Life and Letters of Charles Darwin*, pp. 533–34.

Chapter 5: Modern Acceptance and Rejection of Darwinian Evolution

49. Ernst Mayr, *One Long Argument: Charles Darwin and the Genesis of Modern Evolutionary Theory*. Cambridge: Harvard University Press, 1991, pp. 162–64.

50. Quoted in Robert W. Cherny, *A Righteous Cause: The Life of William Jennings Bryan*. Boston: Little, Brown, 1985, p. 173.

51. Excerpts from bills quoted in Cherny, *A Righteous Cause*, p. 122.

52. Quoted in Ray Ginger, *Six Days or Forever?: Tennessee v. John Thomas Scopes*. New York: Oxford University Press, 1958, p. 7.

53. Bowler, *Charles Darwin*, pp. 203–204.

54. Bowler, *Charles Darwin*, pp. 217–18.

55. Tim M. Berra, *Evolution and the Myth of Creationism: A Basic Guide to the Facts in the Evolution Debate*. Stanford: Stanford University Press, 1990, p. 144.

For Further Reading

Isaac Asimov, *In the Beginning.* London: New English Library, 1981. Asimov, one of the great "explainers" of the twentieth century, devotes part of this volume to the origins of life, providing a very clear explanation of the theory advocated in Darwin's masterwork.

L. Sprague de Camp and Catherine C. de Camp, *Darwin and His Great Discovery.* New York: Macmillan, 1972. This excellent volume explains the intricacies of evolutionary theory in very understandable language.

Walter Karp, *Charles Darwin and the Origin of Species.* New York: American Heritage, 1968. A well-written overview of Darwin's thesis about the evolution of higher life-forms from lower ones, including sections about the controversy the book originally generated.

Jerome Lawrence and Robert E. Lee, *Inherit the Wind.* Originally produced on Broadway in 1955. Reprint, New York: Bantam Books, 1982. This is the intellectually stimulating and highly entertaining play based on the Scopes trial, which revolved around the lawfulness of teaching Darwin's theory of evolution in public schools. The authors changed the names of Bryan, Darrow, Scopes, and other main characters but retained the essence of the proceeding, including close paraphrases of many of the lines from the actual court transcripts. I also strongly recommend the 1960 film version of *Inherit the Wind,* directed by Stanley Kramer and starring Spencer Tracy and Fredric March (available on videotape). Tracy and March, two of the greatest American film actors of the century, deliver spectacular performances in the Darrow and Bryan roles, respectively, and the whole film is gripping throughout. The 1988 TV version, with Kirk Douglas in the Bryan role, is adequate but does not compare to the earlier movie.

Don Nardo, *Charles Darwin.* New York: Chelsea House, 1993. A detailed but easy-to-read overview of Darwin's life, including his early interest in nature; the famous voyage of the HMS *Beagle,* in which he gathered evidence that would later buttress his evolution theory; how that theory developed; the writing of the *Origin of Species;* the controversy following the book's publication; and Darwin's later writings and endeavors.

Works Consulted

Primary Sources

Charles Darwin, *Autobiography,* in *Autobiography and Selected Letters.* Edited by Francis Darwin. New York: Dover Publications, 1958; and *The Autobiography of Charles Darwin: With the Original Omissions Restored.* Edited by Nora Barlow. New York: Krause, 1969. Darwin's autobiography contains much fascinating information about his life and researches.

————, *The Descent of Man.* New York: Random House, n.d. This follow-up to *The Origin of Species* deals with human evolution, which Darwin maintains is part of a random, undirected natural process.

————, *Early Notebooks.* Transcribed by Paul H. Barrett, in *Darwin on Man,* edited by Howard E. Gruber. New York: E. P. Dutton, 1974. A collection of some of Darwin's many notes, which he took when observing plants and animals in the wild.

————, Selections from Darwin's *The Journal of Researches into the Geology and Natural History of the Various Countries Visited by H.M.S. "Beagle," Under the Command of Captain FitzRoy, R.N., from 1832 to 1836,* and his other writings about the voyage, collected in *The Beagle Record,* edited by Richard D. Keynes. Cambridge: Cambridge University Press, 1979. One of a number of modern books containing a selection from Darwin's *Beagle* journal and his many other writings mentioning that ship's now world-famous voyage.

————, *Letters,* in *The Life and Letters of Charles Darwin,* edited by Francis Darwin. 3 vols. 1885. Reprint, New York: Basic Books, 1959. Darwin's letters to Hooker, Huxley, and many other friends and peers reveal a great deal about his thinking during the more than twenty years during which he worked on his theory of evolution.

————, *The Origin of Species by Means of Natural Selection, or, The Preservation of Favored Races in the Struggle for Life.* 1859. Reprint, New York: New American Library, 1958. Simply put, the greatest and most influential book ever written on the subject of evolution.

Erasmus Darwin, *Zoonomia: or, The Laws of Organic Life.* 2 vols. 1794–96. Reprint, New York: AMS Press, 1974. This work by Charles Darwin's grandfather presents a theory of evolution having much in common with the one outlined in *The Origin of Species;* however, the elder Darwin's version lacks the mass of observable evidence provided by his grandson.

The Holy Bible (Revised Standard Version). New York: Thomas Nelson and Sons, 1952. As one of the leading characters in *Inherit the Wind* (the famous play about the Scopes trial) says: "It's a great book; but it is not the only book."

Lucretius, *The Nature of the Universe*. Trans. Ronald Latham. Baltimore: Penguin Books, 1951. The Roman philosopher Lucretius quotes or paraphrases some of the writings of the Greek thinker Empedocles, who proposed a brilliant theory of evolution in ancient times.

Charles Lyell, *Principles of Geology*. 1830–33. Reprint, New York: Straechert-Hafner, 1970. Lyell's great book about the workings of the natural world had a profound influence on Darwin and other nineteenth-century scientists.

Alfred Russel Wallace, *Darwinism: An Exposition of the Theory of Natural Selection*. New York: AMS Press, 1975. Wallace, who concocted a theory of evolution strikingly similar to Darwin's, here summarizes his colleague's ideas.

Philip Wheelwright, ed., *The Presocratics*. New York: Macmillan, 1966. Contains numerous quotes from the works of ancient Greek scientists, including Anaximander, who suggested that humans evolved from fishlike creatures.

Major Modern Sources

J. H. Bennett, *Natural Selection, Heredity and Eugenics*. Oxford: Oxford University Press, 1983. A detailed synopsis of modern evolutionary theory.

John Bowlby, *Charles Darwin: A New Life*. New York: W. W. Norton, 1990. One of the best of the many available biographies of Darwin.

Peter J. Bowler, *Charles Darwin: The Man and His Influence*. New York: Cambridge University Press, 1990. Bowler, a noted science historian, explores how Darwin's ideas influenced other scientists. Highly recommended.

———, *Evolution: The History of an Idea*. Berkeley: University of California Press, 1989. Another excellent volume by Bowler, this one explains how the theory of evolution itself evolved over time, beginning with the ancient Greeks.

John L. Brooks, *Just Before the Origin: Alfred Russel Wallace's Theory of Evolution*. New York: Columbia University Press, 1984. The fascinating story of how Wallace proposed his own theory of evolution at the same time that Darwin was doing preliminary work on *The Origin of Species*.

Ronald W. Clark, *The Survival of Charles Darwin: A Biography of a Man and an Idea*. New York: Random House, 1984. A very readable biography of Darwin, including clear explanations of many of his ideas and an excellent bibliography.

Richard Dawkins, *The Blind Watchmaker: Why the Evidence of Evolution Reveals a Universe Without Design*. New York: W. W. Norton, 1987. This brilliant, informative book explores the notion of evolution as a random, purposeless process. Somewhat difficult reading for those uninitiated in the subject, but well worth the effort.

Daniel C. Dennett, *Darwin's Dangerous Idea: Evolution and the Meanings of Life*. New York: Simon & Schuster, 1995. A fine overview of the theory of evolution as proposed by Darwin in his *Origin of Species*.

Adrian Desmond and James Moore, *Darwin*. New York: Warner Books, 1992. A well-written general synopsis of Darwin's life and work.

Ray Ginger, *Six Days or Forever?: Tennessee v. John Thomas Scopes*. New York: Oxford University Press, 1958. A very fine, readable, and dramatic telling of the infamous Scopes "monkey" trial.

Bentley Glass et al., eds., *Forerunners of Darwin: 1745–1859*. Baltimore: Johns Hopkins University Press, 1968. This scholarly book contains long, detailed, informative essays by leading experts about Maupertius, Lamarck, Erasmus Darwin, and other important proponents of evolution who preceded Charles Darwin. Will appeal to serious students of the subject only.

David L. Hull, *Darwin and His Critics: The Reception of Darwin's Theory of Evolution by the Scientific Community*. Cambridge: Harvard University Press, 1973. Hull does a worthy job of collecting a wide range of material about the reactions to and debate over Darwin's masterwork in the immediate years following its publication.

William Irvine, *Apes, Angels, & Victorians: The Story of Darwin, Huxley, and Evolution*. New York: McGraw-Hill, 1955. A spirited overview of the relationships among Darwin and his scientific colleagues. Good reading.

Ernst Mayr, *One Long Argument: Charles Darwin and the Genesis of Modern Evolutionary Theory*. Cambridge: Harvard University Press, 1991. Mayr, one of the twentieth-century giants of evolutionary theory, tells how modern scientists came around to Darwin's theory of natural selection after demolishing all other competing theories.

Chet Raymo, *Skeptics and True Believers: The Exhilarating Connection Between Science and Religion*. New York: Walker and Company 1998. A very informative and entertaining book about how creationists and scientists find themselves at odds in the modern world.

Carl Sagan, *The Dragons of Eden: Speculations on the Evolution of Human Intelligence.* New York: Ballantine Books, 1977. The late, great Sagan, one of the best scientific explainers of the past century, delivers a thought-provoking excursion into the realm of human evolution and race memory. Fascinating reading from start to finish.

————, *Shadows of Forgotten Ancestors: A Search for Who We Are.* New York: Random House, 1992. A fine overview of the saga of modern science in its quest for the origins of life and intelligence.

Additional Modern Sources

George Basalla, *Victorian Science.* Garden City, NY: Doubleday, 1970.

Tim M. Berra, *Evolution and the Myth of Creationism: A Basic Guide to the Facts in the Evolution Debate.* Stanford: Stanford University Press, 1990.

Robert W. Cherny, *A Righteous Cause: The Life of William Jennings Bryan.* Boston: Little, Brown, 1985.

Theodore H. Eaton Jr., *Evolution.* New York: W. W. Norton, 1970.

R. B. Freeman, *Charles Darwin: A Companion.* Folkstone: Dawson, Anchor Books, 1978.

Stephen J. Gould, *Ever Since Darwin: Reflections of Natural History.* New York: W. W. Norton, 1977.

————, *The Panda's Thumb: More Reflections on Natural History.* New York: W. W. Norton, 1982.

Robert M. Hazen and James Trefil, *Science Matters: Achieving Scientific Literacy.* Garden City, NY: Doubleday, 1991.

Gertrude Himmelfarb, *Darwin and the Darwinian Revolution.* New York: W. W. Norton, 1959.

Leonard Huxley, *Charles Darwin.* London: Watts, 1921.

————, *Life and Letters of Thomas Henry Huxley.* 2 vols. New York: Appleton, 1900.

L. J. Jordanaova, *Lamarck.* New York: Oxford University Press, 1984.

Walter Karp, *Charles Darwin and the Origin of the Species.* New York: American Heritage, 1968.

Desmond King-Hele, *Erasmus Darwin.* New York: Scribner's, 1963.

Edward Lurie, *Louis Agassiz: A Life in Science.* Chicago: University of Chicago Press, 1960.

Tom McGowen, *The Great Monkey Trial: Science vs. Fundamentalism in America.* New York: Franklin Watts, 1990.

Alan Moorehead, *Darwin and the Beagle*. New York: Harper and Row, 1969.

Desmond Morris, *The Naked Ape: A Zoologist's Study of the Human Animal*. New York: Dell, 1967.

Nocolaas A. Rupke, *Richard Owen: Victorian Naturalist*. New Haven: Yale University Press, 1994.

Michael Ruse, *But Is It Science?: The Philosophical Question in the Creation/Evolution Controversy*. Buffalo, NY: Prometheus Press, 1988.

Steven M. Stanley, *Earth and Life Through Time*. New York: W. H. Freeman, 1986.

William B. Turrill, *Joseph Dalton Hooker: Botanist, Explorer and Administrator*. London: Scientific Book Guild, 1963.

Robert Wesson, *Beyond Natural Selection*. Cambridge: MIT Press, 1991.

Gerhard Wichler, *Charles Darwin: The Founder of the Theory of Evolution and Natural Selection*. New York: Pergamon Press, 1961.

G. M. Young, *Portrait of an Age: Victorian England*. London: Oxford University Press, 1973.

Index

Picture Credits

About the Author

Historian Don Nardo has published many books for young adults about the history of science and new scientific discoveries, including *Greek and Roman Science, Dinosaurs: Unlocking the Secrets of Ancient Beasts,* and *Medical Diagnosis.* He has also written extensively about Charles Darwin, the theory of evolution, and the Scopes trial. Mr. Nardo lives with his wife, Christine, and dog Bud in Massachusetts.